GENDER DIVERSITY AND NON-BINARY INCLUSION IN THE WORKPLACE

GENDER DIVERSITY AND NON-BINARY INCLUSION IN THE WORKPLACE

The Essential Guide for Employers

Sarah Gibson and J. Fernandez

Jessica Kingsley *Publishers*
London and Philadelphia

First published in 2018
by Jessica Kingsley Publishers
73 Collier Street
London N1 9BE, UK
and
400 Market Street, Suite 400
Philadelphia, PA 19106, USA

www.jkp.com

Library of Congress Cataloging in Publication Data
A CIP catalog record for this book is available from the Library of Congress

British Library Cataloguing in Publication Data
A CIP catalogue record for this book is available from the British Library

ISBN 978 1 78592 244 2
eISBN 978 1 78450 523 3

Printed and bound in Great Britain

MIX
Paper from
responsible sources
FSC
www.fsc.org   FSC® C013056

Disclaimer

Throughout this book current law, with particular regard to UK law, is discussed and its relation to non-binary people. To the authors' knowledge, all information regarding this is correct at the time of publication. No material in this book should be taken as legal advice given by the authors Sarah Gibson and J. Fernandez, by any organizations the authors represent, by the publishers Jessica Kingsley Publishers or anyone else otherwise named or referred to in this book. Advice in this book regarding the law should be considered solely the views of the authors unless otherwise noted.

Acknowledgements

The authors would like to thank Sam Hope (Hope Counselling and Training), Dr Jos Twist, Lee Gale (Gendered Intelligence), Simon Croft (Gendered Intelligence) and Vic Valentine (Scottish Trans Alliance) for contributing their time, experience and skills to the creation of this book. Their help has been invaluable.

Contents

Non-Binary Inclusion

Welcome to *Gender Diversity and Non-Binary Inclusion in the Workplace: The Essential Guide for Employers.* In this book we will be guiding you through the process of making your organization inclusive of non-binary people. While society has made great strides in recent years to becoming a more open and friendly place, it still remains harsh and unforgiving to many people who are targeted simply for being themselves. Non-binary people are one of these groups, still waiting to be afforded many civil rights that most would take for granted. The purpose of this book is to break new ground – to be the first book of its kind to tackle many of the issues non-binary people face. We hope that after reading this you will have a better understanding of non-binary people and that you will know how to make your organization more inclusive.

As media coverage around transgender people has increased, so too have the number of people asking questions: How are trans people challenged in society, and what sort of issues do they face? Could any of my friends or colleagues be trans? How do I feel about trans issues? While individuals have been challenging how they think about gender, organizations have been working to respond to the needs of all trans people, including non-binary people. Powerhouses like Facebook and HSBC have thought about inclusion and what it means, introducing new policies and outward displays of appreciation of gender diversity. Not only in the UK or the US, but worldwide, LGBT+ and trans-specific organizations have been working to ensure transgender people are included in workplaces, government legislation and everyday life.

Non-binary people – those who don't fit into the categories of men or women – are often a forgotten 'subtype' of trans people. While many organizations are fantastic at making sure trans people are supported and are helpful in facilitating transitions, including offering support for coming out, taking time off for medical treatment and making a switch to a different name or uniform, there are complexities which non-binary people face that trans men and women often don't. For example, how do you record an employee's gender if they're not a man or a woman? Does a trans support group automatically include a non-binary person? What does it mean when a member of staff wants to go by the pronoun 'ze'?

All of this, and many more questions, are things that employers may need to consider when recruiting people, thinking about new equality and diversity policies or when a member of staff might come out as non-binary. It helps to be prepared and to think about these questions ahead of time, rather than being forced to react in haste. Moreover, even if an organization thinks it doesn't have non-binary members of staff, formulating a policy for including non-binary people can help to improve the workplace for all employees.

We have aimed to make this book accessible to as wide a range of people as possible. We begin by introducing you to the basics of who non-binary people are and what daily life is like for them. We then move to the workplace, giving you an overview of UK law, considering why you should make your company inclusive of non-binary people and, most importantly, how you can achieve this. Discussions of non-binary people are frequently carried out in an academic style, but we have attempted to make this book as jargon free and as practical as possible. While we have focused on the UK, the majority of the book applies worldwide.

This book is aimed at human resources professionals or anyone responsible for equality and diversity within an organization, but the tools and practices it teaches are relevant to everyone. If you don't know what the word non-binary means, this book is for you. If you already know the basics of what it means to be non-binary, but want to learn how to better support non-binary people, this book is for you too. If you are a non-binary person and want help and support within the workplace, then this book is also for you.

Making this world a better place benefits us all. We are excited to travel this journey with you.

Diversity strategy

Before beginning with the substance of our subject matter it is worth setting out how we intend to approach the process of greater inclusion and how the information we provide fits in with this. When looking at the inclusion of different groups some areas are significantly more mature than others, for example, work surrounding race and ethnicity or women's rights. By this, we mean that many of the basic premises are widely understood and long-term plans and monitoring schemes have been established. With growing areas, such as our own, there has been a need to take people from no knowledge to a better understanding or to replace misconceptions and stereotypes.

What naturally follows from this situation is the question of 'How can we do better?' Tied in with this is a set of rigid minimum standards imposed by law. As a result, inclusion guidance in growing areas has tended to suffer from two problems: of supplying too much and largely irrelevant information to the reader, with little practical help; or providing formulaic advice that has encouraged generic approaches.

Diversity is largely a dynamic, rapidly changing sector being fuelled by our growing interconnectedness and the willingness of people to explore and articulate new ideas. A strategy for improving diversity and inclusion must match this; in essence it must be a process of continuous learning.

What we do not intend to do is to provide a set of templates for policies or processes for you to use. What we will do is: introduce some of the basic premises; discuss why inclusion is beneficial; give you a snapshot of the current knowledge about the key issues and UK legislation; and provide some practical pointers on where to start change. We will attempt to walk the tightrope between too much and too little information, between being too abstract and too simplistic.

If there is one message to keep in mind while you are reading this book it is this: you won't learn everything about non-binary people from reading this book, and neither would we be able to tell you all there is to know, for we, ourselves, are still learning.

Chapter 2

An Introduction to Non-Binary People

Who are non-binary people?

What does it mean to be a man or to be a woman? You might think that is a somewhat odd question to ask in a book specifically about non-binary people or that the answer is just so plainly obvious that it isn't worth taking the time to ask. The vast majority of people will never have thought in any great detail about why they are the gender they are or, more importantly, why they are not some other gender, which makes it an excellent starting point for us.

We don't put much thought into our gender because the answer has been embedded into our lives. We are socialized into our roles throughout childhood, divided by our gender and taught what we can and cannot do and how we can and cannot act. No only do we copy how adults act, we are given active encouragement through phrases such as: 'that's not very lady-like' or 'boys will be boys'. In later life we tend to subconsciously reproduce the same messages we have absorbed. You can find these subtly in adverts, in the way characters in films or in novels speak or even in the way we interact with each other. From the emphasis that is put on parents to find out and celebrate the gender of their baby, hold pink or blue baby showers, buy certain toys and disregard others, to the reinforcement of separate and distinct genders through school uniforms and stereotypes (girls can only join the netball team, and all the boys are expected to like football), the idea that there are only men and women surrounds us through life. This is what we refer to as the 'binary', the idea that there are only men and women, and there is nothing outside of this.

If pressed for an answer on what it means to be a woman or man, some may start by listing off stereotypes: men are strong and women are pretty and social. A cursory glance around in a public place will likely find you someone who doesn't fit that stereotype, as probably will a glance into a mirror. So, we need to broaden our categories a little.

What about our bodies or sexual organs, do these determine your gender? People who reject the idea of non-binary identities may recruit 'science' to describe why people can only adhere to the categories of men and women; chromosomes, anatomy, brain structure and sex hormones are employed to slot us into one box or another whether we like it or not. But is this really the case? Biology tends to be a major stumbling block for people, mainly because we don't really teach each other very much about our own biology, just enough to get on with our daily lives without being too concerned about what's going on under our skin. We all believe that our own bodies match one of the two templates we were shown: we have an XX or an XY chromosome pair, plenty of oestrogen or testosterone and a set of primary and secondary sexual characteristics to match.

In reality, when we have a few billion humans each with a few trillion cells in their bodies, things tend to be a little more messy. For example, genetic sexual characteristics are determined by the interactions of many chromosome pairs, but even the most well-known one (XX and XY) can come in variants such as XXY or XO and many more. Sex hormones get similarly complicated, with different kinds and different levels as well as how receptive we are to each of them, as does the structure and function of our reproductive organs. We term people with these physical variations 'intersex', because they are different from what society considers typically male or typically female bodies and they account for around 1 per cent of the population. It is important to note that not all intersex people are non-binary and not all non-binary people are intersex; being intersex relates to a person's physical characteristics at birth and this has no bearing on who is non-binary.

Ultimately, biology should not be a factor in deciding who is legitimate. Nobody routinely tests their chromosomes or hormones, and secondary sex charac-teristics should never be used to judge a person's worth. Anyone would find it dehumanizing to have their most intimate details probed and scrutinized and it is just as wrong to apply this to a trans or non-binary person as to a cis person – a person who is not trans and whose gender matches their sex assigned at birth.

So, if we have variations in biological makeup and in our gender expression, what makes someone a woman or a man? The answer is that it is the best description of who they are and it best fits how someone experiences themselves and how they interact with the world. Non-binary genders are an extension of this, a broad category term for those whom the terms 'man' or 'woman' don't fit completely or don't fit at all. Just as there is more than one way to be a man or woman, there is more than one way *not* to be a man or woman. In fact, there are a whole lot of ways and as many gender identities to match.

It is also important for cis people to recognize the ways in which the gender binary fails them. Many cis people transgress the gender binary and norms: from drag performance to women breaking historical and social boundaries in the face of sexism to parents refusing to reveal the gender of their baby straight after birth. It is not just trans people who would benefit if society were to become more flexible and open to the idea of multiple genders; a shift of this kind would be of benefit to all people.

Non-binary people are an exceptionally diverse group although, unfortunately, this gets overly simplified into incomplete taglines, such as describing them as people who are 'both or neither men nor women, or some other third gender'. How people describe being non-binary varies greatly, just as people's individual experiences do, but it also varies between different cultures around the world. Terminology changes between countries and cultures: the term 'genderqueer' is popular in the US as a synonym for non-binary but has a more restricted meaning in the UK; the term 'third gender' is more common in Asia; and there are also a number of culturally specific words.

Non-binary people are simply people trying to get on with their lives in a way that makes them happy. What makes someone non-binary is easier to understand than some people would have you believe, with many wanting to challenge their validity through an incomplete understanding of biological or social variations. What makes someone non-binary is the same as what makes someone a man or a woman – it is simply what suits that person best.

Are non-binary people transgender and do they transition?

Knowledge about transgender people has become much greater and more accepted over recent years but has largely been focused on binary trans people. Non-binary people don't necessarily identify as being transgender, although between a third (Titman 2014b) and two-thirds (Valentine 2016a) do.

Specific support and inclusion practices for non-binary people are still lacking and much of the guidance relating to transgender people is insufficient to cover non-binary people's needs. Practices for including transgender people will still mostly be helpful in including non-binary people and much of the guidance in this book will similarly be useful for supporting binary trans people. The two strands currently work in parallel with much overlap, but both sections are needed for a complete picture.

The reasons a non-binary person may or may not identify as being transgender are varied and only complicate the issues, so we shall not discuss them. It is merely sufficient for our purposes to know that there is overlap between being non-binary and being transgender, but being one does not necessarily imply the other.

Non-binary people do share many of the experiences of binary transgender people. Some may experience gender dysphoria, a medical diagnosis originating from people treating you and your gender differently from how you would like to be treated, just as some binary trans people do. Some may seek medical interventions related to gender dysphoria or change their names or appearance to better suit themselves. These processes are all elements of a transition process and guidance on how to support non-binary people through this will be given later on.

Transition for all trans and non-binary people can be made up of both social and medical aspects: social elements include changes to one's name, style of dress or how others address you, while the medical elements might include interventions to make changes to a person's body, surgery or counselling support. None of these are required to be trans or non-binary and many people feel that these are unhelpful to them. There is a historical trend in outdated guidance giving an overly detailed and voyeuristic description of medical transition processes but, instead, we will only be focusing on this in a practical manner, with regard to how it affects other parts of a person's life.

Common non-binary genders

We've touched on the fact that non-binary people are actually a diverse group, and that the term itself is somewhat of a catch-all, describing anyone who isn't solely a man or a woman. One of the common questions from those wishing to learn more about being inclusive of non-binary people is 'What are all the non-binary gender identities and do the differences matter?'

There are a lot of non-binary genders, too many for a person to comfortably learn, and this list is ever expanding. Don't worry, you don't need to learn every gender identity in detail and we ourselves certainly haven't. The way we structure our recommendations later in the book should work for all non-binary people.

It is, however, worth taking the time to understand some of the more common gender identities and to learn some of the words or themes that crop up more frequently. This is to aid a deeper understanding and allow you to talk about non-binary people in a way that will assure them that you know what you are talking about.

Some of the most common themes people employ when describing their gender identity are:

- being more than one gender

- switching between distinct genders intentionally or unintentionally

- not having a gender

- not finding gender a useful term to describe themselves

- knowing they are not one particular gender but being unsure as to what they are

- generally being unsure or still exploring.

While these are common themes, it is more important to focus on how someone describes their own gender identity and it would be wrong to think of someone in terms of these themes. Knowing the common terms people use is also important and we've summarized the most common ones used in the UK in Figure 2.1, based on a study by C. Lodge in 2016 for the Nonbinary Stats blog (Nonbinary Stats 2016). This summary is far from exhaustive, but should cover most of the ones that you'll hear.

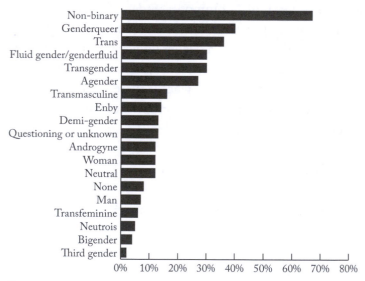

Figure 2.1: Usage frequency of non-binary genders

When talking about non-binary people, you shouldn't simply list a number of these gender identities as it appears that you are giving priority to some over others and also, it simply gets much too long to read. Instead, we use the term 'non-binary' to cover all of these gender identities, as it is the most commonly accepted term in the UK.

As part of our work we have looked at some of the more commonly used gender terms for non-binary people today, collecting non-binary people's descriptions of their own gender(s) (Beyond the Binary 2015b). In this and below can be found some of the more common words we found that people in the UK are using to describe themselves, and what they mean.

Non-binary

Many non-binary people can't or don't want to limit their understanding of gender to a 'subcategory', and are more comfortable just saying they are generally non-binary.

'I am not a man or a woman, but somewhere between the two. I think.'

'Neither male nor female, somewhere in between or outside of the binary genders.'

Genderqueer

Genderqueer is a more political term, prevalent in the US, where it acts as a substitute for non-binary, and tends to be used by younger non-binary people. Whereas queer has been used by lesbian, gay and bisexual activists to own their sexuality, genderqueer can often be used as an upfront statement about how the nature of someone's identity challenges the norm.

'Otherwise third gender, non-binary. Just not male or female.'

'In between "male" and "female" somewhere, but fluctuating in that space.'

Agender, gender neutral, neutrois and a general lack of gender

These terms are commonly used by people who feel they have no gender and that none of the terms or ideas that go with gender have relevance to them. In general, these people prefer to see themselves in terms of their own unique experiences.

'I don't feel I have an innate gender. Gender, for me, personally, is just about gender expression and how people perceive me.'

'I feel like other people have a little compass somewhere inside themselves which points to their gender; some people have more than one needle in their compass, some people's needles move around over time, etc. I don't have a compass.'

'A lack of identification with deemed "masculinity" or "femininity".'

'No attachment to any form of gender; they're just kinda there but something that affects other people, not me.'

Genderfluid

Being genderfluid describes a state of flux or switching between genders, either male or female, or different non-binary genders. Many non-binary people have a fixed sense of gender, that is, they can be agender all the time, or genderqueer all the time, with no change. Some non-binary people do change, either depending on the situation, or day to day or week to week.

'Gender can be anywhere from male to female and in between.'

'My gender fluctuates between masculine and feminine, including agender and androgynous. It may change on a day-to-day basis or remain the same for weeks on end. As such, I choose gender-neutral pronouns.'

'A gender identity that seems to change fluidly. My overarching gender would be genderfluid, but "subgenders" can change over time to feel more masculine or feminine or agender or some combination.'

Demi-gender

A person with a demi-gender may be part or mostly one gender and part of or mostly another. For example, a demi-boy may be someone who is mostly a boy, but can be part of something else.

'70 per cent girl, 10 per cent boy, 20 per cent Something Mysterious.'

'A bit of fluidity (mostly seen in presentation and dysphoria level/presence) within a fixed, fairly narrow range between fairly-femme and neutral-ish.'

Cultural-specific genders

There have been places around the world for thousands of years that have recognized, and continue to do so, the existence of genders outside of men and women. The idea that gender is partially cultural and reinforced by the history we grow up with and the gender roles we create becomes clear when we learn about gender variance in different societies globally. Some indigenous American nations recognize and value 'two-spirit' people, a sacred and spiritual role incorporating male and female elements. Mahu is a Hawaiian term for a third gender in Kanaka Maoli (Hawaiian) and Maohi (Tahitian) cultures. These people were, and are, reflected in art, song and stories, although negative attitudes towards third gender people were brought in by Christian colonizers. Closer to the Western world, we have always found historical accounts of gender fluidity in ancient pagan ritual. Saxo Grammaticus (c.1150–c.1220) was a Danish historian, theologian and author, and documented ritual gender transgression in the cult of Freyr in Uppsala, Sweden. In his work *Gesta Danorum*, legendary Norse hero Starkad resides there, where he 'had become disgusted with the womanish body movements, the clatter of actors on the stage and the soft tinkling of bells' of male priests during fertility rituals. What is common is that, in many societies, a tie has been made between breaking gender boundaries and spirituality; non-binary people can be seen as more in tune with the spiritual world as the performers of valued rituals and keepers of special knowledge.

It is important to note that some terms popularly used by non-binary or trans people in the West may be considered offensive in other countries, and also that some terms are specific to a culture or region. For example, a person who is not an indigenous person of a nation where the term 'two-spirit' is used cannot legitimately co-opt this phrase to describe their identity, as it is directly tied into the history and culture of a certain group of people. In other countries, trans people, who many may consider to be 'binary' trans men or women, would cross over into a culturally specific gender identity; for example, the hijra of Pakistan may also be or identify as trans women, and indigenous Australian brotherboys may also be or identify as trans men. Acknowledging this is to understand the extent of the fluidity of gender and gender categories globally, and to realize that our understanding of the rigid binary categories of man and woman doesn't extend to all people across history or the world.

How an individual experiences and defines their non-binary identity will be unique to them. No two people will have the same definition of what it means to be 'agender' or 'demi-gender', just as no two people will have the same definition of what feeling like a woman or a man is like. Nobody expects non-trans people to memorize or learn by rote definitions of gender terms; this is not where respect for a person lies. The most important thing you can do, even if you aren't sure exactly what a person means when they describe their gender, is to accept them for who they are, and treat them with the same validity you would any other person.

Pronouns and titles

All English users will know what a pronoun is and will regularly use them, although few will have had cause to think about them in detail. It will come as a disappointment to our linguistically inclined readers, although others will likely breathe a sigh of relief, that we will not be delving into a rigorous discussion of grammar here. That said, the use of pronouns is an important part of non-binary people's lives.

Pronouns are words such as 'he', 'she' or 'they', which can act in place of a person's name. For example, 'my friend went to the shop and s*he* bought... ' with *she* replacing the friend's name. Importantly, the pronouns 'he' and 'she' can indicate the gender of the person to whom they are referring. The pronoun 'they' is more complicated and can refer to a plural group, 'my friends went to the shop and *they* bought...' 'They' can also refer to a single person without attaching gender to them, 'my friend went to the shop and *they* bought...' This makes the singular 'they' a gender-neutral pronoun.

Now, as with many discussions about grammar, there are those who are fervently opposed to the usage of 'they' to refer to a single person even though they will still be able to understand what it means when it is used, most likely without even noticing its presence. In fact you would not have made it this far into the book if you did not understand a singular 'they', since we have already used it 21 times in this book. The singular 'they' has been a part of the English language for hundreds of years, being found in the works of William Shakespeare and Jane Austen, appearing in the style guides of many newspapers and magazines and being listed in the Merriam Webster dictionary. In contrast to the historic use of the singular 'they', the honorific 'Ms' is a relatively new addition to the language (as it was revived in the 20th century) but is widely accepted.

Some non-binary people choose to be referred to using gender-neutral pronouns as it would be incorrect to attach a male or female gender to them using 'he' or 'she'. This isn't the case though for all non-binary people and some may actually prefer 'she' or 'he'. Similarly, some non-binary people may have more than one pronoun which they find acceptable or prefer one pronoun on some days and another one on other days. There is no one-size-fits-all approach here and it is important to refer to people as they would like.

A portion of non-binary people wish to be referred to using gender-neutral pronouns but don't feel that the singular 'they' is correct for them. A number of new pronoun sets have appeared to fill this gap and can seem quite alien when seen for the first time. Table 2.1 lists some of the more common gender-neutral pronouns and their declension. You are most certainly not expected to memorize these, but it is important to know of their existence and to use them if asked. If you are having trouble with getting these right, then a non-binary person will almost certainly be happy to help you if you are making a genuine effort to use them.

Table 2.1: Declension of pronouns used by non-binary people

	Nominative (subject)	Oblique (object)	Possessive determiner	Possessive pronoun	Reflexive
Traditional pronouns					
He	He is laughing	I called him	His eyes gleam	That is his	He likes himself
She	She is laughing	I called her	Her eyes gleam	That is hers	She likes herself
It	It is laughing	I called it	Its eyes gleam	That is its	It likes itself
They	They are laughing	I called them	Their eyes gleam	That is theirs	They like themselves
Non-traditional pronouns					
E (Spivak, 1983)	E is laughing	I called Em	Eir eyes gleam	That is Eirs	E likes Emself
Per (Piercy, 1979)	Per is laughing	I called per	Per eyes gleam	That is pers	Per likes perself
Thon (Converse, 1884)	Thon is laughing	I called thon	Thons eyes gleam	That is thons	Thon likes thonself
Xe (Rickter, 1973)	Xe is laughing	I called xem	Xyr eyes gleam	That is xyrs	Xe likes xemself
Ze, hir (Bornstein, n.d.)	Ze (Zie, Sie) is laughing	I called hir	Hir eyes gleam	That is hirs	Ze (Zie, Sie) likes hirself
Ze, zir (unknown, c.2013)	Ze (Zie, Sie) is laughing	I called zir/zem	Zir/zes eyes gleam	That is zirs/zes	Ze (Zie, Sie) likes zirself/zemself

In C. Lodge's non-binary statistics survey of 2016 (Nonbinary Stats 2016), a question was included about the most common pronouns non-binary people use both worldwide and in the UK, as shown in Figure 2.2. Unsurprisingly, the most favoured pronoun was the singular 'they' (78.8%). Behind that were both the binary pronouns of she and he, with the option of pronoun mixing coming in fourth place. Results for the UK and worldwide were quite similar, showing similarity worldwide in pronoun usage generally.

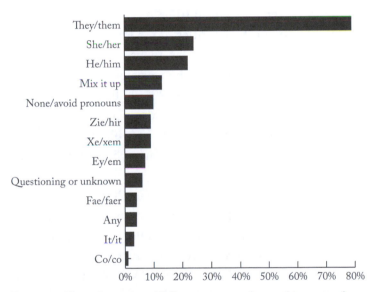

Figure 2.2: Usage frequency of different pronouns by non-binary people

Titles – honorifics used when addressing somebody formally – are elements that convey gender to people immediately, without knowing a person's pronouns, or even their name. Even when an individual has a gender-neutral name, such as 'Sam', some people may use the presence of a title to determine the gender of the person.

To change a title, you don't need to go through any formal process, and anybody can use standard titles such as Mr, Miss or Mrs, as well as the gender-neutral title, Mx. Organizations and institutions should be able to update titles on request; however, some titles are controlled by law (for example, Dr, Professor or Sir). The only drawback may be IT systems that do not currently have the capability to do this and this is a situation non-binary people often encounter when trying to change their title to a gender-neutral option. However, many organizations have since updated online forms and databases to reflect the need for gender-neutral titles.

As the majority of titles do confer gender, many non-binary people may prefer to use a gender-neutral title. While there are several in existence, as shown in Figure 2.3 (Nonbinary Stats 2016), by far the most common one is 'Mx', which avoids specifying a gender. Not only is this title used by some non-binary people, but also by binary trans or cis people who simply don't want to use a gendered title.

First used in the 1970s (Titman 2014a) and rising to popular usage among trans people in the decades following, Mx is one of several gender-neutral titles in circulation, and is commonly pronounced 'Mix' or 'Mux'. Other variations include 'M.' or 'Misc.', standing for miscellaneous, and even 'Ind.', short for 'individual'. It is worth noting that, as shown in Figure 2.3, a significant number of non-binary people prefer to use no title as opposed to Mx, believing titles to be redundant. Others may want to use a title such as 'Dr', as this is already neutral and accepted, and would be inclined to opt for a career or qualification that would mean they could use another neutral title. Some may also choose to switch titles depending on the situation, similar to usage of pronouns.

More and more organizations are adopting processes to allow customers to select a gender-neutral title. One prominent example is the HSBC bank, which adopted vMx along with nine other titles that customers can use. Other institutions that accept the title 'Mx' include the Driver and Vehicle Licensing Agency (DVLA), the National Health Service (NHS), the Universities and Colleges Admissions Service (UCAS) and local councils. With the growing media coverage about businesses becoming more open to the idea of gender-neutral titles, it is likely that more and more will follow suit.

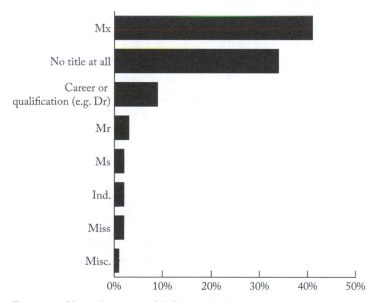

Figure 2.3: Usage frequency of different titles by non-binary people

How many non-binary people are there?

Many people assume that non-binary people are rare and that they are unlikely to meet a non-binary person, although many people will have met a non-binary person without realizing it. While they comprise a relatively small segment of the population there are still significant numbers of non-binary people. It may come as no surprise that there is limited accurate data on the prevalence of non-binary people, both worldwide and for the UK. This is owing to the fact that UK census data does not include non-binary people (yet) and any surveys of non-binary people are small in sample size. The Australian Bureau of Statistics included the option of an 'other' gender in the 2016 census and there have been similar proposals in New Zealand, ahead of their 2018 census. These moves will help to build a better picture of the numbers of non-binary people around the world in the future.

In the UK, work by N. Titman in 2014 (Titman 2014b) estimated that there may be up to 250,000 non-binary people in the UK, which equates to 0.4 per cent of the UK population. While Titman discusses the issues in the data sizes, this is one of the closest estimations we have of the size of the population of non-binary people in the UK. For comparison, a survey in 2009 by the Equality and Human Rights Commission (Aspinall 2009) found at least 0.6 per cent of people in the UK identify as bisexual, and census data shows that 0.4 per cent are Jewish and 0.4 per cent are Buddhist (Office for National Statistics 2011). The figure of 0.4 per cent of the population as a whole being non-binary has been found in other pieces of large-scale research, such as the Equality and Human

Rights Commission's survey of over 10,000 people in 2012 (Glen and Hurrell 2012).

This number will likely continue to rise as knowledge and acceptance of non-binary people increases. Younger people tend to be more represented than older people in the non-binary population as they are connected to a more diverse group of people through social media and youth organizations. For example, a study by J. Walter Thompson Intelligence in 2016 found that 56 per cent of Generation Z in the US knew someone who used gender-neutral pronouns compared to 43 per cent of millennials. A similar situation can be seen in relation to the wider trans population with greater recognition leading to a sharp rise in the number of trans people.

Unfortunately, the lack of non-binary legal recognition or non-binary gender options in census surveys makes it hard to accurately measure the number of non-binary people in a country. We can say that there are more non-binary people than one might expect, and that their numbers will likely rise significantly over the next decade.

Chapter **3**

Key Issues

Like trans men and women, non-binary people face significant levels of discrimination in society. As well as daily life reinforcing the fact that there are only two rigid gender options non-binary people face big hurdles, many of which cause physical and mental harm. These include the lack of legal gender recognition, which comes with many associated challenges, the limits of social identification, and the rigid gender binary being present in many aspects of daily life. In this chapter we'll be discussing the most pressing issues facing non-binary people, to give you a glimpse into what life looks like as a non-binary person.

Barriers to healthcare

Similar to trans men and women, access to healthcare and medical practitioners' understanding of trans issues is 'hit and miss'. While there are fantastic resources produced by trans groups to educate medical professionals, such as nurses and staff in GP surgeries, this has still not translated into an inclusive and supportive healthcare system. Research by the Royal College of General Practitioners Northern Ireland (RCGPNI) in 2015 found that '74% of trans people report at least one negative experience [in general health services] and 20% do not avail of general health services at all'. While the guide produced by the RCGPNI is a good step forward in the education of GPs, there is no reference to non-binary people aside from a brief mention in a glossary of terms.

Many non-binary people, like trans men and women, report the 'trans broken leg' phenomena; as soon as they go to seek medical help for one unrelated issue, their trans status will be the sole fixation of a medical professional, to the detriment of any other mental or physical health issues. This deters them from going to see doctors and compromises their healthcare.

Even some gender identity clinics (GICs) in the UK, where trans people are referred to for transition-related treatment, remain rooted in the binary idea that it is better to only treat trans men and trans women. A minority still believe that non-binary people are more likely to 'detransition' or regret receiving medical help, despite there being no evidence of this.

Non-binary people have, in more recent years, vented their frustration with a limiting trans healthcare service, which can often be discriminatory or ignorant of non-binary people, through the Twitter hashtag campaign #transdocfail. Stories from the Action for Trans Health website (2014) and the *Non-Binary Experiences of Healthcare* survey (Action for Trans Health 2015) highlight the fact that some of the staff working to treat trans people still buy into binary descriptions of gender, rather than seeing trans individuals as people with varying means of gender expression:

'Was refused transition treatment for being lesbian, riding motorcycles, and not wearing skirts and heels to appointments. #TransDocFail'

'Initially I was told that I would not be endorsed for any treatment unless I presented as a binary-identified person and followed a prescribed (binary) treatment "pathway". I was referred by the GIC for cognitive behavioural therapy and blocked from seeing GIC clinicians during this time.'

In our 2015 #SpecificDetriment survey (Beyond the Binary 2015a) we collected some non-binary people's experiences of trans-specific and general healthcare, finding similar issues to those raised through the #transdocfail social media discussions:

'[I] had to pay for my own trans-related medical expenses (around £5,500), since I couldn't access them on the NHS, because of being outside of gender binary. [I had] doctors refusing to understand or respect me, inappropriate comments, lack of awareness/care of my health needs.'

'My hormones were delayed another 4–5 months since I had to have another GIC appointment because I was non-binary.'

'I feel acutely dysphoric when I have to be in hospital and it's a difficult thing to deal with when care workers visit to help cater for my disability. I'm terrified of being stuck in a care home where my gender isn't respected.'

A survey conducted by the Scottish Transgender Alliance in 2016 detailed non-binary people's experiences of using UK GICs; again, the message was clear, saying that '...there were mixed feelings among respondents about whether they felt comfortable to share their non-binary identity' and indicating that '...over half of participants did not feel comfortable sharing their non-binary identity the majority of the time' (Valentine 2016b). While this means there is still work and further training to be done with GICs, many non-binary people do report having positive interactions with clinicians.

While non-binary people have a large number of negative experiences with regard to accessing trans-related healthcare, GICs in the UK do help non-binary people with physical transition, as WPATH (World Professional Association for Transgender Health) guidance has recommended. Revisions made to the WPATH guidance in 2011 sought to expand the understanding of gender, moving away from a historical focus on trans men and women to a recognition that trans people who fall into a wider range of identities may want to seek medical transition (WPATH 2011).

Daily life

As we have mentioned in previous chapters, existing as non-binary in a society that, by and large, refuses to acknowledge the presence of more than two genders, is mentally and emotionally draining for many non-binary people. Despite the slow social recognition of non-binary people through articles on gender, characters in TV shows and more awareness of trans rights generally, there are often specific 'microaggressions' that non-binary people face every day. Coined by Harvard University professor Chester M. Pierce in his 1970 work 'Offensive Mechanisms', a 'microaggression' referred to the daily racist comments he witnessed towards Black people; the meaning now extends to encompass the daily comments, slights and barriers that any marginalized group faces. Microaggressions are not hate crimes, which we will also look at in this chapter, but are incidents so commonplace that they wear down individuals and can have lasting impact. Below are some common ones that non-binary people face in their everyday life.

Misgendering and mispronouning

The use of gendered pronouns is often a source of microaggressions for non-binary people. We often assume, based on physical appearances and other traits, what someone's pronouns are and that they are either 'he' or 'she'. Many non-binary people use a gender-neutral pronoun, such as 'they', but as gender-neutral pronouns are not commonly used, many non-binary people are 'mispronouned' (have the incorrect pronoun used for them) on a daily basis. This also links in with 'misgendering', or assuming someone's gender incorrectly. Of course, there are incidents where mispronouning or misgendering is accidental, although, unfortunately, some people have a strong resistance to the idea of non-binary genders. These people are often eager to wilfully misgender or mispronoun someone, either through laziness or to prove a point that they should fit into either binary gender.

There are many ways that you can be mindful of using the wrong pronoun for someone or misgendering them. Little steps can include offering pronoun stickers alongside name badges if in a conference or meeting, or explaining where male, female and accessible bathrooms are if someone asks for them, rather than guessing which ones they'd like to use.

'I asked a [workshop] facilitator to use non-gendered pronouns with me and two colleagues put in a complaint saying it made people uncomfortable.' (Fernandez, Gibson and Twist 2017)

'I was afraid of making people feel uncomfortable, or the possibility that rather than address me or refer to me wrongly, they would just ignore me. Hence, I said that they can call me "she" so that it is easiest for all.' (Fernandez *et al.* 2017)

Language

Language is central to our ideas about gender. The words 'man' and 'woman' are just as much a construct of our gender landscape as 'non-binary' or 'genderqueer'. Just as new words are being added to people's colloquial use every year, so are new terms to describe people's genders. Language is, like society, gendered. Examples are prevalent in the US, where 'ma'am' or 'sir' follow many statements by customer service agents. Even in the UK, the phrase 'ladies and gentlemen' often precedes a public announcement. Small incidents like this often go unnoticed by cisgender people; however, for non-binary people, who are often attuned to gendered language, by way of being erased by it, it can be a reminder that there is no place to fit into. Small adjustments in speech can make a difference to a non-binary person's day; perhaps they are tired of being called 'sir' all day, and a checkout assistant instead, saying 'thank you, have a good day' can mean a lot. Being mindful of language is similar to being mindful of people's pronouns and gender; it is a learning process, and small steps can be a gradual way of introducing the idea of being open to more genders.

'[I am] being constantly misgendered by doctors and other health professionals, even after writing to my GP practice manager to have my sex marker changed to "Not specified" and to ask for my preference for gender-neutral language to be recorded on my medical notes. This results in social dysphoria and anxiety which have on some occasions disrupted my ability to speak coherently about my healthcare needs and concerns, and often make me dread appointments that relate to health concerns with my genitals or breasts.' (Fernandez *et al.* 2017)

'After getting trans awareness training for co-workers at one job, I was then referred to as an "it" when I asked someone not to call me "Madame".' (Fernandez *et al.* 2017)

Recording your gender

For many non-binary people, filling out forms or recording their gender can be a barrier. From everyday applications to important documents, such as medical records, the presence of only 'male' and 'female' options for describing gender forces non-binary people to misgender themselves. Most non-binary people wouldn't mind there being options to record their gender on forms and many wouldn't question if there was a legitimate aim with regard to collecting data about different genders, if only there was an inclusive option. The presence of a box to write in how a person identifies can show a commitment to making sure non-binary people feel included and that recording their gender is important. There is no legal requirement for forms of any kind to adhere to only two options.

'I told HR when I got the job and corrected the title and gender options on the forms I completed, but nothing came of it. I can't be bothered to try and explain it to my colleagues. I think they would try and be understanding and they are fairly right on about LGBT stuff, but they are (as far as I know) all cis and straight and I would feel like they thought I was "weird".' (Fernandez *et al.* 2017)

Single-gender spaces

Non-binary people will always face challenges over accessing single-gender spaces as only options for men and women are provided. From bathrooms to changing rooms, often these spaces will crop up at inconvenient times and force non-binary people to make a choice over which one to use. In the case of store changing rooms, a non-binary person who feels uncomfortable using either may forego buying clothes or shopping all together (31% according to Valentine 2016a). In the case of using bathrooms, non-binary people, and trans people generally, frequently avoid these rather than face potential discrimination or harassment (55% avoid toilets and 42% avoid gyms, Valentine 2016a). It is often on the shoulders of the person in question to inquire if there are gender-neutral options available, whether it's showers or bathrooms at work or private areas in a gym or swimming pool they can use to change. Like language, single-gender spaces are a barrier to non-binary people's participation in daily life and asking for accommodations to be made can risk harassment or ridicule from colleagues at work or service providers.

'My line manager and personnel manager made an effort to get me a locker in the staff canteen so I didn't have to use either of the gendered changing rooms.' (Fernandez *et al.* 2017)

Names and titles

Early on in transition, a non-binary person will often start to use a different name, change their title, or look to amend gender markers on their passport or other documents. There is no such thing as a 'legal name', but many institutions and services still require a legal process in order to recognize any name changes (so despite this not being needed, it doesn't mean it isn't demanded).

While titles have no legal standing in many cases, modifying them can be important to many non-binary people as they imply a gender. A name change via Deed Poll or statutory declaration must always be respected within the workplace, or in any situation where this data is held or viewed.

A non-binary person who prefers to go by a different name may do so without any form of declaration needed. It is also perfectly legal for a trans person to use different names in different places, as long it is not done for fraudulent purposes. It is not uncommon for cisgender people to do this either, that is, to use nicknames or to want to be called by their middle name instead. One way to make a name change official is to apply for a Deed Poll, a legal document that proves a change of name, and which can be used to effect a name change on different official documents such as a passport or driving licence. The only requirements are that a person must: renounce their former name and cease to use it on official documents; not change their name for fraudulent purposes (as mentioned above); or be over the age of 16 (for an unenrolled Deed Poll). All people under the age of 18 seeking a name change must also have the authorization of their parent or guardian to be able to do this, which can mean that those without supportive parents will not be able to do so. In Scotland, a name change via statutory declaration is possible from the age of 16 and over, and under 16 if all those with parental responsibilities consent.

While changing a name is a common occurrence in society, such as moving from a maiden to married surname, for trans people, who may suffer dysphoria at being reminded of their name given at birth, it can be doubly challenging. Every place where you are registered must be contacted and informed of the change of name, and some may require a copy of the Deed Poll to be sent to them, a process that can drag on for months. Despite a formal change of name, some institutions can refuse to accept it or intentionally do not make the change correctly, for example, by adding their new first name as a middle name or not updating the title. This is considered discrimination and it frequently begins a prolonged process where a non-binary person has to explain the details of the law in order for the change to be made correctly. This still remains a common occurrence and places a huge burden on non-binary people.

Titles are not usually legally binding, and there are no official steps a non-binary person has to take to change them. This applies to common titles, such as Mr, Ms, Mx or Miss, but not to others that are conferred honours, such as Dr, Lord or Sir. For a person to request a title change, all they would need to do is say so, either verbally or in writing.

Hate crime

In 2015, the Ministry of Justice (MoJ) responded to a petition hosted on the Petition Parliament website which called for the right of trans people in the UK to self-define their legal gender (Petitions UK Government and Parliament 2015). The response sparked outrage from many trans people and trans activists online, particularly regarding the last paragraph of the response statement, which focused on the question of making legal documents inclusive of non-binary gender options. On the continued exclusion of many non-binary people from the legal gender recognition process, the MoJ said:

'The Equality Act 2010 protects people from discrimination if it arises from their being perceived as either male or female. We recognise that a very small number of people consider themselves to be of neither gender. We are not aware that that results in any specific detriment, and it is not Government policy to identify such people for the purpose of issuing non-gender-specific official documents.'

We know that this isn't the case. Non-binary people face specific marginalization that runs throughout every aspect of daily life: in finding work and in workplaces, accessing healthcare, harassment on the street and even discriminatory treatment at GICs.

In submitting evidence to the Women and Equalities Committee inquiry into trans inclusion in 2016, James Morton, from the Scottish Trans Alliance, said:

'We are aware that the Ministry of Justice said there is no specific detriment faced by non-binary people. In our survey of 895 non-binary people in the UK, within the last five years, 11% said they had been refused services and one third had experienced harassment in services. In employment within the last five years, one fifth had experienced workplace harassment and 95% were worried about disclosing themselves as non-binary in the workplace and being discriminated against if they came out.' (Women and Equalities Committee 2015)

The MoJ has since acknowledged that their statement, given in response to an online government petition to allow the self-determination of gender, caused offence among many non-binary people. Our previous work in 2015 has collected instances of how non-binary people are discriminated against in everyday life, from healthcare to employment. This showed that non-binary people, as well as not being afforded legal recognition in the UK, have to contend with barriers to vital services.

As part of this, we asked non-binary people if they feel comfortable or safe living as non-binary in the UK. This question also asked about mental health as well as physical safety, and whether living as non-binary in the UK had an effect on both. The results were shocking and upsetting, with non-binary people being the victims of hate crime, harassment and rape, based on their gender or gender presentation. Many non-binary people, unsurprisingly, reported high levels of anxiety and depression (Beyond the Binary 2015a):

'I have frequently been harassed in the street, on transport etc., over my gender presentation. People will hold debates with their friends over whether I'm a boy or a girl, I've been called slurs including tra***, f***** and d***, and physically pushed out of gendered toilets (both men's and women's; I've had to resort to using disabled toilets).'

'I used to live in South Wales, I did not feel like it was safe for me to transition there.'

'I've been physically assaulted in the street and raped. I'm scared I'm going to die because I am non-binary. I can't do anything with my life any more. I want my daughter to do things, go places, but I'm too afraid to take her places, I fear for her safety if she is seen with me.'

'I have been harassed, shouted at, and had objects thrown at me from moving cars specifically for looking androgynous (visibly non-binary), not for being perceived as male or female as is covered under discrimination legislature. Street harassment based on looking non-binary or being visibly trans is far worse in the UK than in other countries I have lived in and visited.'

A hate crime is defined in UK law as any incident which the victim, or anyone else, thinks is based on someone's prejudice towards them because of any protected characteristic under the Equality Act, including race, religion, sexual orientation, disability or because they are transgender. Sometimes, a hate crime is obvious: physical assault or being verbally abused in the street are common things that trans people report as happening to them when they are victims of a hate crime. But other aspects can be more insidious, such as office 'humour', where the comments are prejudiced or harassing. For example, some non-binary people may express themselves through drag or crossdressing outside of work, something that is often the butt of jokes. Working in an environment where this type of thing is often brought up as a subject of ridicule not only enforces transmisogynistic stereotypes, but creates an unsafe culture for non-binary people.

Ultimately, it is up to the victim of the crime to view it as a hate crime or not; guidance from the police and from advocacy organizations states where a victim is unclear as to what to do they should go with their gut instinct and that if they are uncomfortable with the situation, then they should report it.

While there are figures on the number of reported hate crimes many go unidentified due to the victim's fear of reprisals, or due to the belief that they won't be taken seriously by the police. For example, in the Scottish Transgender Alliance's *Non-Binary People's Experiences in the UK* survey in 2016, 69 per cent of respondents never felt comfortable sharing their non-binary identity with the police (Valentine 2016a).

This figure means that non-binary people experiencing hate crime may well not report it to the police, or may tell the police it was because of another factor, such as perceived sexuality. The Scottish Transgender Alliance recommends that the police should 'ensure that they have training around non-binary identities, and communicate publicly their commitment to tackling hate crime against non-binary people'. These steps towards transparency would make non-binary people feel like they would be taken seriously if they were to report a hate crime.

Unfortunately, the police can often be a barrier themselves. In some cases, the people who are meant to be helping trans people aren't building bridges with the community and are, at worst, perpetuating the same discrimination (Beyond the Binary 2015a):

'Police repeatedly ignored my description of a hate crime as "transphobic" as I do not match their idea of what a trans person looks like.'

'Very little resources exist to help us. Hate crime services usually do not even have the capacity for us to record our genders correctly.'

The Equality and Human Rights Commission only has limited data on the experiences of trans people generally due to the lack of relevant surveys and the difficulty in getting large enough sample sizes to draw conclusions from. However, there is some pertinent data that has been collated by the Equality and Human Rights Commission to draw attention to the levels of hate crime faced by the LGBT community and, specifically, trans people.

A review conducted by the Equality and Human Rights Commission (Mitchell and Howarth 2009) concluded that transgender people experience transphobia in a wide range of forms, including bullying in schools, harassment, and physical and sexual assault. The review also showed that trans people were likely to face rejection from families, work colleagues and friends. Newer research from the Equality and Human Rights Commission in 2015 (Chakraborti and Hardy 2015) on wider LGBT hate crime also demonstrated that there was significant fear of being treated unfairly, leading victims of hate crime to avoid reporting it. In this report, 88 per cent of LGBT people had experienced a hate incident. Another study by Whittle, Turner, and Al-Alami (2007) found that 40 per cent of transgender respondents had experienced verbal abuse, 30 per cent had experienced threatening behaviour, 25 per cent had experienced physical abuse and 4 per cent had experienced sexual abuse.

These studies show that there is no question as to whether trans people face a high level of hate crime. Recent figures from the *Independent* have put the rate at almost trebling in the past five years (Yeung 2016). It is likely that many non-binary people are included alongside trans men and women in reporting these incidents.

However bad the figures might be, there are always organizations that work to help non-binary people report hate crime, and do advocate on their behalf to get their reports taken seriously. Through advocacy offered by organizations such as Galop, non-binary people experiencing hate crime can choose to remain anonymous, or have another person report on their behalf, meaning that they may feel the risk of repercussions is lessened to an extent. Other services offered include things like helping someone to move if a neighbour or community is the cause of harassment, providing information on privacy rights and help in applying for compensation in case of injury from a crime. It is very important that employers are aware of the support systems in place to help trans people report incidences of hate crime. Making all staff aware of how to report hate crime means that the pressure to liaise with the police is not just on the victim's shoulders and that there can be a collective responsibility if there is a fear that a colleague is being subjected to hate crime. More information can be found on Galop's website (www.galop.org.uk).

Chapter 4

UK Law Background

While the UK has made significant strides with regard to inclusion for binary trans people, in many areas it is unclear as to how protected non-binary people are. Whereas some non-binary people do take steps to transition, other non-binary people do not, and they may feel unsure of how they fit into protective legislation. In these situations, it is usual practice to assume that non-binary people are covered unless specified otherwise; however, this lack of certainty leaves non-binary people questioning their inclusion regardless. Our previous work (Fernandez *et al.* 2017) has found that non-binary people have very little confidence that they are protected under current equality legislation; 57 per cent are either unsure of their protections or believe that they are not protected at all in the workplace, and this figure rises to 61 per cent with regard to them being protected as consumers. In both cases only 1 per cent answered that they felt the law completely protected them.

This section will give an overview of the most pertinent points in UK law as it applies to non-binary people, including how they relate to the wider trans community, and any issues that arise from them. This will not be legal advice but, rather, the current understanding of the law will be outlined. It is important to note that, as much of the law is a grey area for non-binary people, there are groups in the UK working to create further changes with regard to legal recognition and the status of non-binary people. Employers who wish to go above and beyond to create a safe and inclusive environment for all employees should take note of current legislation when it comes to gender recognition and see if changes or adjustments need to be made in the workplace.

Equality Act 2010

One of the most frequently cited pieces of legislation with regard to the protection of non-binary people within the law is the Equality Act 2010 (chapter 15). This was the first Act that gave trans status a 'protected characteristic', meaning transgender people cannot be discriminated against, harassed or victimized, and should have equal access to employment, education, goods and services.

Useful examples of discrimination under the Equality Act can be:

- Obtaining goods or services – where a person is denied access to goods or services because of a protected characteristic. This is often one of the most recognized forms of direct discrimination. One example of this could be a non-binary person who appears to be dressed androgynously not being served in a restaurant, with the manager telling them that they don't serve 'their kind' here, telling them they 'need to be appropriately dressed'.

- Recruitment – it is direct discrimination for anyone to be denied a job because they are trans or non-binary. An example might be a non-binary job candidate asking for feedback following a job interview in which they mentioned they were trans but were rejected, with the interviewer making it clear that they would not be a good fit for the company due to their gender presentation and use of gender-neutral pronouns.

- Promotion at work – non-binary people may be passed over for promotion, where as cisgender colleagues may be looked upon more favourably. This also extends to training opportunities, which must be made available to employees regardless of gender.

- Harassment – defined as any unwanted behaviour linked to a protected characteristic that violates someone's dignity or creates an offensive, intimidating, hostile, degrading or humiliating environment for them. This includes protection for a person being impeded from performing their job properly.

- Victimization – where a person is treated unfairly because they have complained about discrimination or harassment or helped someone else to do so. For example, it would be discrimination to view a non-binary person as 'troublesome' because they have reported harassment.

The Equality Act covers both indirect and direct cases of discrimination. Indirect discrimination is where a rule, practice or procedure is applied to everyone, but disadvantages people who have the protected characteristic. Conversely, direct discrimination is discrimination based on the knowledge or perception that a person has a protected characteristic, or on a person being associated with a person with the protected characteristic. An example of indirect discrimination might be a uniform policy that is gendered; while this rule is applied to everyone, it makes some non-binary people uncomfortable and excluded.

The Equality Act also introduced a broader public sector Equality Duty. This gives public bodies legal responsibilities for taking proactive measures to address equality. It means that organizations such as the NHS, prisons, schools and other organizations that receive public money have to foster good relationships between different groups of people and ensure all groups have equal opportunities to access services.

The wording of the Act mentions that the protected status is one of 'gender reassignment' and covers any person who 'is proposing to undergo, is undergoing or has undergone a process (or part of a process) for the purpose of reassigning the person's sex by changing physiological or other attributes of sex' (Women and Equalities Committee 2015). Such a person is referenced to as a 'transsexual person' under the Act, which is a descriptor that many trans people feel is outdated and inaccurate.

While the Act, at its first conception, was lauded as a major breakthrough for trans protection in law, there have been increasingly more and more vocal criticisms of the specific wording, which may unintentionally discriminate against non-binary people. Generally, a lot of trans people feel that centring the process of 'gender reassignment' and being 'transsexual' is unnecessarily focusing on physical transition and a normative process of transition (from female to male or vice versa). This will not be the case for many trans people, and despite a trans person not undergoing any physical transition, the Act will still apply. This means that employers and other service providers may assume wrongly that the only people covered fully by the Equality Act are those who have fully undergone 'gender reassignment', or who are holders of a Gender Recognition Certificate (GRC) (see Gender Recognition Act 2004; Chapter 7). At the Women and Equalities Committee's inquiry into trans discrimination and challenges in the UK (Women and Equalities Committee 2016), experts proposed new wording to make the Act more inclusive, changing 'gender reassignment' to 'gender identity', meaning an end to the ambiguity on the status of non-binary individuals once and for all.

While this is one change that may be made in the foreseeable future, employers should note that non-binary people are currently covered by the protections of the Equality Act, either by having the protected characteristic of gender reassignment or being perceived to have it. For example, if a non-binary person came to their manager at work and said they were thinking about asking other colleagues to start using gender-neutral 'they' pronouns for them, they would be protected under the Act. This would be considered to be a proposal for undergoing a process for reassigning the person's sex – so the protections are actually very wide. Despite the wording being imperfect, this is not a reason to assume that discrimination against non-binary people is acceptable at work.

Data Protection Act 1998

The Data Protection Act 1998 (Chapter 29) is one that most employers will be informed about. This relates to the protection of people's personal information: obtaining it, usage and what can be legally kept on record and for how long. Under the Act, trans status and gender reassignment are categorized as 'sensitive data'; therefore, information relating to a person's trans status may not be kept on record or transmitted to another party unless the conditions for processing sensitive data are met. More information on the guidelines can be obtained from the Information Commissioner's Office (ICO).

To summarize, in order for an organization to comply with the Data Protection Act, sensitive data:

- must not be shared externally without permission from the individual whose data it is and evidence of that permission should be kept

- should be marked appropriately and kept separately to other data, so only people who need to access the data may access it by using passwords or some other form of encryption

- should only be shared internally with a good reason

- should be accurate and as up to date as possible

- should not be kept longer than necessary.

Every person has the legal right to inspect their data held by institutions. This means a non-binary person has the right not only to ensure necessary data about their trans status is held under the processing safeguards with regard to sensitive data, but also has the right to learn what is being held about them and make changes or request that the data is removed and destroyed.

Gender Recognition Act 2004

The purpose of the Gender Recognition Act is to change a person's legal gender marker recorded on their birth certificate. The GRC exists only for the Gender Recognition Panel to instruct the registrar of births, deaths and marriages to make a new entry in the register, from which a new birth certificate is issued. The Act also protects an individual's privacy, as it ensures gender reassignment status cannot be disclosed. Gender change can also affect what level of pension a trans person is entitled to (see Chapter 6).

In fact, as all other legal documents can be changed without a GRC (e.g. NHS records, a passport and a driving licence), many trans people never obtain one. While it was considered to be a significant achievement at the time it was brought in, the certificate is now considered to be outdated by many in the trans community.

Obtaining a GRC can be a drawn-out process, and one which many trans people choose to bypass, simply because of the work and fees involved. It requires a trans person to jump through hoops and submit 'evidence' to a Gender Recognition Panel, who remain anonymous and whom the submitter will never meet. The panel will then make a decision based on the paper evidence whether a person will be issued with a certificate or not if the criteria have not been met. For a long time, the mysterious nature of the panel and the medicalization of the transition process have created a culture of apprehension for trans people, who may not have typical transition narratives or who may not want to seek physical transition. The emphasis on the 'legitimacy' of receiving a psychiatric diagnosis from the NHS when one may not be wanted can also put pressure on already stretched GICs.

Upon giving evidence at the Women and Equalities Select Committee, James Morton, from the Scottish Transgender Alliance, explained how distressing the panel's approach can be for applicants. His organization had supported:

'a number of trans people who have been really traumatized and humiliated by the process where they have [had to say whether they have] undergone various medical treatments. The Act says you should be able to access your gender recognition without necessarily having those, and yet the gender recognition panel has insisted on really intrusive levels of detail about the surgeries that people have undergone or their intentions for future surgery. We have had, for example, a young person in their early 20s who has not yet had any sexual relationships being forced to decide and state categorically whether or not they want genital surgery and being questioned over the fact that initially they wanted breast augmentation but then grew breasts through hormone treatment. Panels have been incredibly pedantic about any perceived inconsistencies in the medical reports, which means that people end up extremely upset and feel really invalidated.' (Women and Equalities Committee 2015)

If a trans person does acquire a GRC, then all information regarding their previous gender must be destroyed. An employer is not allowed to ask to see a GRC, or allowed to record having seen one; employers will only come into contact with GRCs if a trans person chooses to present one to them. Also, if a person has a GRC, it is illegal for an employer to disclose their trans history for any reason if this has been found out in an 'official capacity'.

Unfortunately, there remains no provision for the recognition of non-binary identities under the Gender Recognition Act, or for anyone under 18. If a non-binary person did want legal recognition under the Gender Recognition Act, as either male or female, there is a risk that they would be denied this on the basis of their gender identity; however, some have opted for this.

Legal recognition

Non-binary people in the UK are still not able to have their gender recognized under UK law. While transgender men and women can change their 'legal' sex by applying for a GRC, non-binary people cannot do the same as the option to choose a non-binary identity or no gender is not permissible. Despite calls for the Gender Recognition Act to be reformed to be inclusive of non-binary people, the UK government has ignored these. A 2015 petition to Parliament to allow trans people the right to self-define their gender obtained 35,000 signatures, enough to draw a response from the MoJ (Petitions UK Government and Parliament 2015). Despite many challenges to this position during the Women and Equalities Committee Transgender Equality inquiry, the government's stance has not changed; non-binary genders are still not recognized in UK law, and trans individuals can only become legally recognized by the state as male or female by obtaining a GRC. On the petition page, a government spokesperson responded:

'Non-binary gender is not recognized in UK law. Under the law of the United Kingdom, individuals are considered by the state to be of the gender that is registered on their birth certificate, either male or female.'

'Under the Gender Recognition Act, the Gender Recognition Panel is only able to grant a certificate to enable the applicant to become either male or female. The Panel has no power to issue a certificate indicating a non-binary gender.'

'The Equality Act 2010 protects people from discrimination if it arises from their being perceived as either male or female. We recognise that a very small number of people consider themselves to be of neither gender. We are not aware that that results in any specific detriment, and it is not Government policy to identify such people for the purpose of issuing non-gender-specific official documents.'

Unfortunately, legal recognition for non-binary people under the Gender Recognition Act remains a future development, with no timeline as to when or if it might be delivered by the current government.

Why is non-binary recognition important?

Why is non-binary legal recognition so important to people? Surely gender is only a marker on a form anyway, and now that men and women are equal in nearly all respects under the law, is having your gender correctly recorded really necessary? Do non-binary people feel so strongly about birth certificates that the entire framework of gender recognition has to change?

The truth is both tangible and psychological for many non-binary people. Knowing that there will always be a record of an undesired gender on your official documents can still be a source of dysphoria for non-binary people, even many years down the line. A non-binary person may still be apprehensive in showing a passport or driver's licence as a form of proof of identity, just like a trans man or woman may be apprehensive in showing proof of identity if their gender marker has not been changed. In turn, this may affect many areas of a non-binary person's life; it can out them as being non-binary. It means, in turn, that getting a job is harder when you don't want to out yourself, or you can be subjected to misgendering, or have to deal with difficult conversations with a potentially ignorant employer. It is the reason that non-binary people cannot get married as the gender that they are. All of this means that non-binary people often have no choice but to hide who they are in many areas of their lives, for fear of conflict and not being taken seriously. Having proof on official documentation that a non-binary person is recognized as the gender they are can help to de-escalate situations of conflict, make non-binary people feel safer or just give them a sense of mental comfort.

With no option to correct official documents where gender is mandatory, non-binary people can be stuck in a limbo between two ill-fitting options, as either 'male' or 'female' would be wrong.

Non-binary recognition on official documents is something that the majority of non-binary people want. In the Scottish Transgender Alliance's *Non-Binary People's Experiences in the UK* report (Valentine 2016a), '64% of [survey] respondents would like to have their legal gender/sex on official documents (including birth certificates, passports and drivers' licences) recorded as something other than "male" or "female", 16% were unsure, 14% would like to change it on some documents but not others, and 6% do not want this option'.

The reasons given for this in the report were similar to those cited above:

'If there became an option to have non-binary legal recognition, more people might stop dismissing non-binary gender identities because it will be on a legal document!'

'Legal recognition at least makes it possible for people like me to be part of society, to not be on the outside. It is also the best step forward towards more social acceptance and integration of non-binary identities.'

On the other hand, some non-binary people feel that the way forward isn't to 'add in' non-binary legal recognition, but to redefine as a society what recording legal gender means. Is it right that it should be mandatory on certain documents to record gender, and does it serve a purpose? Some non-binary people feel that instead of adding non-binary legal gender markers and perhaps encouraging disagreement on these, it would be best to do away with the process of recording gender.

The same report also contained responses from non-binary people who remained critical of steps towards 'official' inclusion, wondering if moves would be performative, with no real reduction in hate crime or social recognition of non-binary people:

> 'I really think fundamentally questioning whether/ why we need a "legal gender/sex" is really important and I wouldn't want it to be overlooked in favour of making more of them exist and changing how/whether they're recorded on documents. We have no notion of a "legal name"; we just have names that we use and are known by, and these can be changed at will, provided you take whatever steps necessary to satisfy the various bureaucracies you deal with in your day to day life. Why then is "legal gender/sex" such a mess?'

> 'I don't know if this really means anything beyond a surface-level acceptance. What does this do to actually improve the material conditions of non-binary people?'

The reasons for and against the legal recognition of non-binary gender on official documents, and what the best next steps should be, are debated even among non-binary people. What is important is that, for many, the thought of a way to be officially recognized is comforting and would be a way to alleviate dysphoria created by living in a society that refuses to recognize on paper anything other than men or women. While legal recognition is not in place, individuals and organizations who want to support non-binary people can do so by remaining sympathetic to the discomfort non-binary people experience when asked for any proof of identity that includes a gender marker. Recording gender privately is not subject to the law, so there are ways of holding accurate descriptions of employees' genders on file through modifying databases and adhering to the Data Protection Act. Being open with a non-binary employee and making it clear that they will be treated according to their wishes, regardless of what is 'official', can put their minds at ease and make society fairer for all.

Other countries

While the UK leads the way on many LGBT+ protections, it may come as a surprise that in terms of legal recognition for non-binary people, other countries are doing better. In a 2015 statement by WPATH, a message of solidarity with non-binary people was communicated:

'Legally recognized documents matching self-identity are essential to the ability of all people to find employment, to navigate everyday transactions, to obtain health care, and to travel safely; transgender, transsexual, or gender-nonconforming status should not preclude individuals from enjoying the legal recognition all citizens expect and deserve.'

The WPATH *Standards of Care for the Health of Transsexual, Transgender, and Gender-Nonconforming People*, Version 7 (2011) recognize that there are a number of gender identities, and 'that choices of identity limited to Male or Female may be inadequate to reflect all gender identities: an option of X or Other (as examples) may be advisable'.

Some countries have evidently taken this guidance and the guidance of local and national trans rights groups on board, and have taken steps to ensure non-binary people can have legal documents issued in the correct gender. For example, in New Zealand, Australia and Denmark, passports with 'X' as a sex descriptor have been available from 2012 for trans people. In Nepal, the Supreme Court ordered the government to issue citizenship ID cards that allow 'third gender' and 'other' to be listed. The court recommended that the only requirements to identify as third gender would be the person's own self-identification (*Sunil Babu Pant and Others v Nepal Government and Others* 2007):

> 'Legal provisions should be made to provide for gender identity to the people of transgender or third gender, under which female third gender, male third gender and intersexual are grouped, as per the concerned person's self-feeling.'

Similar provisions for a third marker on citizenship ID and voter registration cards also exist in India, Pakistan and Bangladesh.

Malta has a gender recognition law that is regarded as being the gold standard in the world. Under the Gender Identity, Gender Expression and Sex Characteristics

Act 2015, applicants can change their gender identity documents by simply filing an affidavit with a notary, eliminating any requirement for medical gender reassignment procedures.

In addition, in 2017 in the US, an Oregon circuit court ruled that a resident could legally change their gender to non-binary. The Transgender Law Center believed this to be the first ruling of its kind in the US (*The Daily Dot* 2017). California also recognizes non-binary people, and a bill is currently going through their Senate to establish how this works in practice for state ID. There is similar recognition in Washington DC.

Future developments

In the current political climate of change, nobody can be sure what the future will hold for legal developments in trans protection, but there is significant movement on key issues, such as non-binary legal recognition. The UK is fast falling behind Ireland, Denmark, Malta and others who have embraced self-determination for trans people. In 2015, Ireland passed a gender recognition bill that eliminated the need for psychiatric diagnosis in order to obtain legal gender recognition, being only the third country to do this in Europe. So, while there is definitely hope for progress in the UK in the coming years, there must be a commitment from the government to put these actions in place.

As in Ireland, there is significant support for non-binary legal recognition in Scotland and Wales. In Scotland almost all major parties are pledging to introduce non-binary legal recognition and there is vocal support from the current First Minister of Scotland, Nicola

Sturgeon. The Green Party in England and Wales is also vocally supportive of non-binary rights and the respective party leaders have attended Pride celebrations. When changes are likely to be made remains to be seen.

There has been political pressure for a number of years to replace the 'gender reassignment' protected characteristic in the Equality Act with 'gender identity', in order to clear the ambiguous status of some non-binary people's protection under the Equality Act once and for all. At the beginning of 2016, the *Transgender Equality* report by the government's Women and Equalities Committee called for this wording in the Equality Act to be looked at, and for a wholesale review into the needs of non-binary people by the government, 'within six months'; however, despite lobbying from organizations, no concrete plans have been formed. The same is the case with the Gender Recognition Act. The UK government recognizes the need for change based on multiple sources of evidence, but so far lacks any plans to enact it.

Currently, there is no option for a gender marker of anything other than male or female on UK passports. The LGBT equality charity Stonewall recommended in its 2017 manifesto *A Vision for Change* that the UK government should move to include gender-neutral passports as part of a five-year plan towards greater inclusion for non-binary people, enabling them to travel without fear. It notes that the International Civil Aviation Organization allows passports to be issued with an 'X' gender marker, and several countries already have systems in place where it is possible to obtain a passport with a neutral gender marker.

Chapter 5 · · · · · · · · · · · · · · · ·

Why Include Non-Binary People?

Why bother trying to include non-binary people? We hope that, since you've read part way through a book on non-binary inclusion, you are on board with the idea and won't need much convincing, but if you happen to have skipped to this chapter, that is quite all right as well. We know that some people can take a little more convincing and it is well worth taking the time to explain, as it gives us the chance to be a little more optimistic than in previous chapters.

The purpose of this chapter is to answer the questions of 'why?' and 'so what?', particularly from those who have to keep a hawk-like gaze on the bottom line. Our business case will largely be a qualitative analysis because quantitative data, specifically on non-binary people, has yet to be collected, but we will include it where possible.

You might be feeling that this all sounds like a lot of effort to put in for a relatively small segment of the population, but creating inclusive environments has much wider benefits. If there is one message you take away from this chapter, it should be that inclusion is about much more than single groups and that it will have positive effects across the whole of your business.

Recruitment and retention

While, historically, many businesses have overlooked the quality of their intangible assets, much to their peril, human capital is key to the success of any size of business. During the last century, it was far more common for a person to spend their entire working life married to a single company, but this has changed over the last few decades, with workers becoming far more mobile. Competition among firms has intensified both to attract workers from other firms and to retain their own employees in order to maintain or grow a competitive knowledge advantage or to see an improved return on their investment in a person. In the current climate, few organizations are inclusive of non-binary people and this represents a good opportunity for organizations to differentiate themselves from their competitors.

In general, people spend a significant proportion of their time at work and much is said about finding your 'dream job', which is seen as more than just an obligation to perform dull tasks. Less significance is placed on finding your dream employer; however, jobseekers will still need to think carefully about whether the organizational fit is right for them. Job interviews are, of course, a two-way conversation with both the organization and the prospective employee evaluating each other. This is doubly true for a non-binary person, who has to carefully select employers to minimize the chances of being bullied, discriminated against or just hating their job.

As with most things, it is important to discuss this with an eye on the long-term trends. Similar to other equality and diversity areas, non-binary inclusivity has a significant generational divide with younger people more quickly adapting to and embracing emerging issues. This driver has led to universities and schools moving much faster towards being inclusive than traditional businesses, with universities consistently being over-represented in measurements such as Stonewall's (2017a) *Top 100 Employers* (in terms of inclusivity).

Younger people, and recent graduates especially, are far more aware of social diversity issues than their older counterparts and do judge organizations' equality and diversity credentials. In order to attract recent graduates, organizations need to be seen to be moving with the times and be making an effort to be more inclusive.

Our own research (Fernandez *et al.* 2017) on non-binary people's experiences in the workplace and while jobseeking found that 90 per cent of non-binary people would be more likely to apply for a job with an organization that was inclusive. This is pretty much as close to a consensus as you're going to find and, short of just giving everyone a rise or extra holiday, you'll be hard pressed to find anything with such high approval.

Staff retention is obviously influenced by a number of factors, but creating the correct organizational culture is key. A work environment where people are valued, supported and enjoy their work will be one where staff will want to stay. This is the crux of what we are talking about when we say inclusive work environments but, again, it is not just non-binary people who are benefiting. People don't just judge how friendly their workplace is according to their own experiences, but on their perception of how it is supporting others as well. An organization that is visibly investing the time and effort into supporting some of their most disadvantaged staff will be perceived much more favourably than one which is cold and indifferent.

Our research on retention shows that 86 per cent of non-binary people said that they would be more likely to stay with an employer who was inclusive, with 86 per cent again feeling that they would be more likely to enjoy the work. This is fairly easy to understand; when there are so many exclusionary employers out there and the consequences of picking the wrong one are so severe, it is far safer to stay where you are happy than to gamble.

Reducing exclusionary incidents

Unfortunately, exclusionary incidents are very common for non-binary people. Our own work finding is that half suffer an incident in the workplace (45%) or as a consumer (53%) on a monthly or more frequent basis (Fernandez *et al.* 2017). When we look at the causes of these incidents we find that they are very much within the control of organizations, either coming from employees or from specific practices. While this may not currently seem a very positive picture, it does mean that making your organization more inclusive can have a real effect on non-binary inclusion in wider society.

Our research (Fernandez *et al.* 2017) has found that workplace incidents involving non-binary people primarily involve close colleagues (47% of cases) and managers (33% of cases). Such incidents usually involve negative 'jokes' being made or a refusal to refer to someone with the correct name and pronouns. In a few cases, more serious discrimination such as sexual assault occurs. Similarly, when non-binary people are acting as customers, the primary cause of exclusionary incidents was staff members, comprising 86 per cent of incidents, compared to other customers/service users being involved (29% of cases). These incidents commonly included refusing access to a gendered space or service because the staff member did not believe the non-binary person should be allowed access. Either when at work or as customers, the most common groups causing exclusionary incidents are company employees who would be positively influenced by internal training and an inclusive internal culture.

The majority of these incidents do not have complex causes and are usually down to a lack of knowledge and understanding of non-binary people, rather than arising out of malice. It is easy to see why they happen when no help is currently given to staff on how to interact with non-binary people. What is needed to fix this is remarkably simple: a basic explanation that non-binary people exist and should be respected. This would actually go a very long way.

While this guidance is slowly disseminating through the rest of society, by word of mouth or through the media, organizations have the opportunity to accelerate its progress and make a real positive impact. Reducing exclusionary incidents is one of the primary goals for LGBT+, trans and non-binary rights organizations and it is possible for you to be part of the solution. Implementing some basic training for employees, even sharing simple information on who non-binary people are, can have a profound impact on non-binary inclusion across society.

Brand building

Brand awareness and general marketing are important for any size of company but especially for those who sell directly to the general public. In the highly interconnected world of social media it is easy to amplify the quality of adverts and other press stories, with particularly good or bad ones drastically increasing their reach. Being an emotional topic for many, representation of minority groups is a particularly sensitive subject, with an organization's reputation having a large influence on purchase decisions or a person's choice to work with it. Our own research has found that 80 per cent of non-binary people would be more likely to buy products from a company that was perceived as inclusive (Fernandez *et al.* 2017).

In general, it is not overly difficult to generate a positive perception of your organization among non-binary people if due care is taken. Implementing the initiatives that we advocate in this book should provide ample opportunities for a positive press and building a history of being well received by the community. Being careless and not assessing whether any actions would negatively affect non-binary people or minority groups is the most common cause of incidents that would damage an organization's brand. Building an inclusive brand is not as simple as just focusing on what you are doing specifically for those groups, but requires you to think about the impact all of your actions may have. This is an area where it can take some time to build a strongly positive brand but where it is also very easy to damage it.

A recent example of a good article in support of non-binary people that appeared in the press was about a number of high street banks adding gender-neutral titles or neutral genders into their systems. Conversely, an article showing a lack of understanding in relation to such people featured a betting company that invited viewers to guess the gender of cis and trans people as an attempt at a 'joke'. These have become very widely known among the non-binary and trans community, with lasting effects spanning at least several years.

For businesses who sell directly to other businesses, the inclusive aspect of the brand will be less important; however, it is still important not to acquire a negative image. When sales are made between businesses it is not always just goods that are exchanged; the reputations of those businesses become linked by association. For example, a newspaper that sells advertising space to other companies can easily lose deals if it publishes exclusionary or discriminatory content; the companies being advertised may not want their brand appearing alongside such messages or appearing in general with a company that finds such views acceptable. On the flip side, being inclusive can also be used as a differentiator between oneself and the competition.

Inclusive environments are good for companies' output

It is somewhat of a cliché now to say that a happy worker is a productive worker but, nevertheless, it remains true.

Workers who feel supported and happy within a work environment are likely to engage more with their work, generating and sharing their own ideas as well as handling tasks more quickly. This is an all-round boost and while you can have the best talent in the business, if you can't bring it out of people then you are never going to get far. The converse case is even more obvious, that a worker who is dealing with bullying or discrimination will be much more defensive both in not wishing to interact with their co-workers and placing blame on the organization as a whole for allowing such a situation to happen.

While the benefits of an inclusive environment should be clear for non-binary people it also has a wider effect on the whole organization, increasing overall productivity. This is linked to how everyone in an organization perceives and interacts with the organizational culture; all workers feel more supported in a positive culture. This, again, affects workers' willingness to share their own viewpoints and ideas as well as how willing they are to take on and complete tasks. Both positivity and negativity are infectious, with people passing it between each other. It is easy to become locked into a cycle of negativity and creating a successful organizational culture is about ensuring that the cycle remains a positive one.

As part of creating a positive cycle we need to identify and fix anything that is injecting negativity into the atmosphere. The common pitfall is to assume this is tied to a specific person and to remove that person, while it is more common for an organization to draw positivity or negativity from beyond people. The easiest way to maintain a positive atmosphere is to encourage people to be open about any issues rather than to let them fester and escalate, but to do that you have to be effective at remedying any problems that may arise. If everyone feels that an organization is willing to tackle any issues related to discrimination, they will also feel that they can raise other concerns or problems they may have, allowing all issues to be dealt with more quickly.

While non-binary people are usually only a small part of a workforce, the key is in the overall organizational culture because this will affect everyone. Creating a positive culture can be a difficult task to accomplish but focusing on supporting those most at risk is a good way of building an environment that works for everyone.

Legal responsibilities

While it isn't perhaps the most exciting of areas, meeting your legal obligations is essential for any organization. As we have discussed, the way in which equality legislation specifically covers non-binary people is still not currently the most well-understood area, but it is one where there is movement towards greater clarity. Nevertheless, this is a case where it is prudent to assume things are more strict than they are, so we encourage you to cut through the confusion and take it that all non-binary people are fully covered by current equality legislation. If lawyers decide that this is not exactly the case at the moment, then it will likely become so in the near future.

All organizations, public sector ones in particular, have obligations under current equality legislation to ensure that staff are being treated fairly, no matter who they are. The negative side of this, of course, is that organizations allowing discrimination to happen end up becoming liable themselves. Organizations are automatically liable for any discrimination done by their employees or agents, whether they know about or approve of it. Companies are, however, protected if they have taken reasonable steps to prevent employees from discriminating against others. This is usually achieved through giving employees an overview of the law and instructing them not to break it.

Discrimination cases may result in situations where either one or more people are forced to leave, including the victim, who may feel that the environment is no longer safe. More than this, these cases can affect the organization as a whole either through damage to a brand or financially.

The inclusion practices that we advocate should be more than sufficient to meet any legal obligations with regard to non-binary people, both now and in the near future, but they are obviously not meant as substitutes to standard good practices. Through our wider work, we have seen many examples of incidents where the people would have good grounds for a discrimination case to be brought to court. While we don't know of any such cases actually making it to court, it would be wrong to assume that this could not or would not happen even when using current best practice guidelines.

Social responsibilities

The topic of corporate social responsibility is a growing one. Organizations and businesses make up such a large part of our society that they must also play a part in positively shaping it. Largely, the focus of this conversation is currently on the environmental impact of businesses, but other areas are also included, such as paying staff a 'living wage'.

Our topic of interest is whether organizations are helping to promote a more fair and equal society and this is considered of sufficient importance to have parts of this responsibility enshrined into law. While the public sector Equality Duty in the UK applies only to public bodies and those working on their behalf, the principles behind the duty are also relevant to the whole of the private sector. The duty requires that organizations remove barriers and foster good relations with those who have protected characteristics in order to create a more welcoming society.

Meeting legal requirements, however, shouldn't be the end point of a company's objectives, and many believe that they should be doing more. Top companies go beyond the law to support minority groups, pledging their support or putting on events at key times such as Black History Month or LGBT+ prides. This shouldn't be seen as a separate work stream, directly targeting specific groups, but should be a different way of working, being woven into all parts of your work.

Some of the most impressive initiatives we have seen are those which are not highly publicized. These have genuine impact by focusing on supporting charities working for specific groups. This might include, for example, donations of services, allowing them to use your office space or fundraising. While these are good examples of what meeting social responsibilities should look like, we hope you will find your own ways to provide support.

Chapter 6

Practical Steps for Inclusion

Having discussed the 'who?' and 'why?' of non-binary inclusion, we now come to the most important chapter in this book, the 'how?' Throughout this chapter we'll be discussing practical steps you can take to make your organization more inclusive of non-binary people. The majority of these are simple solutions but don't underestimate the impact they can have. The greatest barrier to making an organization more inclusive isn't not knowing what to do, but people within the organization simply not wanting to make changes. In this regard, simplicity is your greatest ally, as is assuring others that any changes won't impact on them. For some of these changes a more active buy-in is required, but we see all of this as a gradual process. The majority of the changes are low effort and if implemented will make you significantly more inclusive of non-binary people.

The remainder of the chapter will be structured around actions and how these will affect non-binary people.

Case studies are included to demonstrate how to tackle any issues that may come up. The case studies are based around real experiences non-binary people have had.

What is important?

We know this section contains a lot of different actions and that some are necessarily going to get prioritized over others, so what are the key things to make your organization more inclusive? When we asked non-binary people to rate the importance of different inclusion measures, there were clear differences in what things mattered to them. Tackling non-binary specific issues such as:

- accepting gender-neutral titles

- having non-binary gender options on forms/records

- having inclusive dress codes

- having gender-neutral bathrooms available and

- using gender-neutral language

were seen as better measures of an organization's inclusivity, while traditional parts of equality and diversity best practice, for example:

- having staff networks

- supporting LGBT+ charities and

- having visible non-binary role models

were viewed far less favourably. This is because the common elements of best inclusion practice are frequently geared towards meeting legal obligations that don't inspire confidence in non-binary people. Otherwise, these elements have not historically covered non-binary people or are completely generic, failing to provide any form of differentiation. While extending your current inclusion policies and practices to cover non-binary people may seem like the easiest route to take, it is far more effective to do this last and instead focus on the issues that are key to non-binary people. How non-binary people rate different inclusion practices is shown in Figure 6.1.

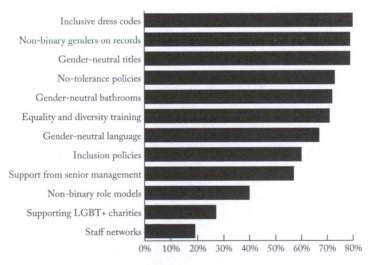

Figure 6.1: The popularity of different inclusion practices among non-binary people

Gender-neutral bathrooms

The subject of bathroom usage has been a long-running issue for trans people and remains one of the most widely and visibly talked about issues today. Put simply, everyone needs to use the bathroom and everyone should be able to do so in comfort. The issue arises when one group claims the other's presence in their bathroom makes them unsafe. We've used the phrase 'one group' intentionally here, because this hasn't historically been an issue of trans vs cis people; it has also played a role in race equality as well as being a lingering issue with regard to sexual orientation inclusion.

Current conversations on this topic usually only focus on binary trans people, with non-binary people included in it by implication, and particularly concern the rights of trans women. The crux of the issue is that some cis women claim to be threatened by the presence of trans women (or men pretending to be trans women), but there has been no evidence to substantiate this claim. The converse, however, that trans women and trans people more widely are at greater risk is, unfortunately, true with trans people experiencing aggression, assault and discrimination whichever gendered bathroom they choose. This can take the form of verbal harassment, physical assault or being denied access altogether.

For non-binary people the issue is slightly more complicated; public bathrooms are commonly gendered, providing separate options for men and women; however, neither of these are aimed at non-binary people and both can be unsafe. A more inclusive solution exists, and this is termed a gender-neutral bathroom, which is one with no gendered signage or segregation. It is commonly thought to have multi-stall units that anyone can enter, which makes both men and women uncomfortable, and women in particular feel unsafe with this scenario.

Most gender-neutral bathrooms are, however, single-stall units and are more common than you would expect. Many small shops will have space for only one bathroom, designated for all customers, and this is an example of a gender-neutral bathroom. You will have certainly used a gender-neutral bathroom in your lifetime as they are common on trains and planes, but by far the most common place to find a gender-neutral bathroom is in a person's own house. While many people are nervous of bathroom formats that they are not familiar with, the number of issues with gender-neutral bathrooms is very low and this does also include multi-stall units.

Gender-neutral bathrooms also have benefits other than for non-binary people, both for a business and all users. Gender-neutral bathrooms are a better utilization of space than gendered ones, as they are available for more people and remove the need to place two gendered bathrooms at every instance. This isn't new knowledge, and small businesses commonly use them where space is constrained. Gender-neutral bathrooms also benefit parents with young children; when the genders of the parent and child differ the choice of which gendered bathroom to use can be awkward. Making the bathrooms gender neutral would entirely remove this problem.

Turning a gendered bathroom into a gender-neutral one is remarkably easy, requiring very little cost; all you have to do is replace the gendered signage with gender-neutral signage. Gendered signage usually features a man or a woman and for gender-neutral signage, we recommend that the sign should display the word 'bathroom' or 'loo' or a picture of a toilet. Note that what are commonly called unisex signs, those featuring both a man and a woman, are not considered gender neutral and should not be used (these only refer to men and women rather than all genders and are hence not gender neutral). The only other issue in making a gender-neutral bathroom is that it is good practice to provide sanitary bins in all gender-neutral bathrooms.

It is worth noting the existence of accessible bathrooms because they are also commonly single-stall gender-neutral units and have operated for a long time without any issues. We do not, however, consider these to be a substitute for standard gender-neutral bathrooms, since they serve distinctly different needs. It is not acceptable to require a non-binary person to use an accessible bathroom if they are not disabled.

What should you do if you cannot implement gender-neutral bathrooms? You should support non-binary people in using the bathroom of their choice and ensure that they remain safe while doing so. If any complaints from other users arise, these should be assessed similarly to how any other person using that bathroom would be; a person's presence in a bathroom is not grounds for wrongdoing and everyone's privacy should be safeguarded, with any acts of harassment or assault treated seriously.

Finally, it is, unfortunately, still common for the issue of bathrooms to be dealt with in an inappropriate way. It is wrong to require a non-binary person to use a specific gendered bathroom based on any physical characteristic of their body or appearance and doing so would be considered discrimination. Gender-neutral bathrooms are for use by everyone, not just non-binary people, and we do not recommend creating another segregated bathroom for non-binary people. Not only would this be an inefficient use of space and resources, but would also highlight who non-binary people are, potentially allowing them to be targeted for discrimination. Relatedly, it is not acceptable to have a segregated bathroom for binary trans people, whose right to use the correct bathroom is protected under the Equality Act 2010.

CASE STUDY

A staff member working in a bar sees a non-binary person, presenting in a mixture of masculine and feminine styles, enter the women's bathroom. A minute later, a woman emerges from the same bathroom and approaches the staff member. She complains that 'there is a man in the women's room' and that the staff member 'should throw him out'. How should the staff member react? The staff member calmly explains that they 'have just been watching and haven't seen any men enter the women's bathroom, but that they saw someone who may be non-binary, who is allowed to be there' and asks if anyone has been 'behaving inappropriately'. The non-binary person has not behaved inappropriately and the staff member reassures the woman that their safety is a priority and should anyone act inappropriately they will deal with it immediately.

Alternatively, if the staff member had not seen the non-binary person enter, they could reasonably go and check. If necessary, they could sensitively let the person know that the bathroom was for 'women and non-binary people'. If the person was non-binary then the staff member should apologize and let that person know that staff will be supportive should anyone bother them.

Gender-neutral changing rooms

Many of the issues in relation to gender-neutral changing rooms are similar to those for gender-neutral bathrooms; however, there are differences with regard to who causes exclusionary incidents. With bathrooms, issues arise from other services users, while in shop settings issues are caused by staff. In these instances, staff deny non-binary people access to gendered changing rooms due to their appearance not matching what they expect from other users. This is, unfortunately, one of the most common sources of exclusionary incidents in consumer environments.

Gender-neutral changing rooms are not common but some have appeared in sports settings, where single cubicles allow anyone to change in privacy. As clothing stores increase the number of gender-neutral clothing lines it is worth considering a move towards gender-neutral changing rooms as well. Otherwise, non-binary people should not be denied access to the changing room of their choice and it is important to train staff to act appropriately. Denying access to a gendered space based on a non-binary person's appearance or physical characteristics would be considered discrimination.

CASE STUDY

A staff member managing womenswear changing rooms hears some people in the queue making derogatory comments about a masculine person who is also queuing for the changing rooms. How should the staff member react? The staff member should approach the people making derogatory comments and ask to 'have a quick word with them' away from the queue. They should explain that they 'can hear the comments that the people are making and that it is unacceptable to treat other customers in this manner'. If necessary, the staff member should go on to say that 'these changing rooms are for anyone wishing to try on the womenswear' and if they 'do not stop' the staff member will 'have to ask them to leave'. If possible, the staff member should apologize to the person for the comments made by the other shoppers.

Records

Systems to record personal information about a person remain a key barrier to non-binary inclusion since these are not designed with non-binary people in mind. Everyone should be able to correctly record their gender and title, but non-binary people are frequently forced to pick incorrect options just to be able to access even basic services such as healthcare. The result of this may be simply being referred to incorrectly or, more seriously, being accused of impersonating someone else. The lack of correct recording of non-binary people makes them invisible within our society and places a huge burden upon them to attempt to have their correct titles and gender recorded.

There is currently no requirement to record non-binary people for equality monitoring purposes; however, updates to the law may well introduce this in the near future. Indeed, when working internationally you may have some contact with countries that do legally recognize non-binary genders and you should be able to record non-binary people correctly if this is the case.

Nevertheless, it is important to record information about non-binary people to monitor the effects of your own equality and diversity work.

The key items to record are:

- titles

- non-binary genders

- a preferred name if different to an official name

- a person's pronouns.

For titles we recommend that a person is given a blank text field to add their own title but, failing that, including the title 'Mx' is also an acceptable option. An option to leave this unrecorded should also be included.

Similarly to titles, non-binary genders are best recorded by allowing a person to fill in a blank field themselves. When this is not possible we recommend the structure:

- male

- female

- non-binary

- prefer not to say.

There is no legal requirement to record a person's legal gender and this should not generally be included. Where it is absolutely necessary to have a binary gender recorded for a person this should be kept separate to the rest of their records. In all cases it should be possible to hide a person's gender record so that it cannot be viewed by all staff. If gender records are not being used for any specific purpose, such as equality monitoring, this information should not be recorded at all.

Preferred names are helpful for non-binary people who have not officially changed their names and this is the name that they should be recorded under. As with legal genders, a person's official name should be kept separate from the rest of their records. Previous names for non-binary people should not be kept if they have fully changed their name and official names should only be kept if the person has not changed their name with other official organizations, such as HMRC. Simply asking for their name to be changed places a requirement on you to change your records of a non-binary person's name and you should not request any form of 'proof' as doing so may be considered discrimination.

A person's pronouns can be helpful to record for contact purposes, but should not be visible to everyone without the person's consent. This field should be used by all employees and not just non-binary people.

All information relating to a person's non-binary status is considered sensitive information under the Data Protection Act 1998 and should not be shared with anyone without the person's consent.

Staff networks

While staff networks are not viewed as the most important measure of a company's inclusiveness of non-binary people, they still add value in larger organizations. Staff networks can promote better cohesion throughout a larger organization, but can also help to support staff and provide a channel through which to raise internal issues. They can be particularly important for groups with relatively few numbers, such as non-binary people.

It is currently very rare to find a staff network that is inclusive of non-binary people as most do not know how to integrate non-binary people into their work. When talking about staff networks it is important to remember that several staff networks may be relevant to non-binary people; LGBT+ staff networks may cover non-binary people more directly, but women's staff networks can be relevant, as many of the issues also affect non-binary people.

To make a staff network inclusive of non-binary people it is important to base this change on the level of knowledge currently in the organization. If you do have non-binary people in your organization it is important to let them lead the change both in the structure and in any activities the network runs. This will help get non-binary people involved and will give you a better-quality network in the end.

If you don't have any non-binary people currently in your organization, or if those there do not want to be involved, then you can involve the staff network in helping to implement other changes we recommend. It is important that they stick fairly closely to our recommendations as they will not have as much experience in these issues, although they can help tailor them to your organization. Running events aimed at non-binary people will also be beneficial, but it is important to acquire knowledgeable speakers and not just general LGBT+ speakers, as understanding of non-binary people, even among LGBT+ people, is generally low. Charities that are non-binary focused are a better option here than non-binary celebrities.

Using gender-neutral language

The language that we use can say a lot about us and we often overlook many of the little subtleties, simply using words or phrases out of habit. For non-binary people the key concern is the usage of gendered terms that are ingrained into how we speak and write English. So common are these that we hear them everyday without even noticing them. However, if an incorrectly gendered word is used to describe you, for example, calling a woman 'sir', then it suddenly becomes jarring and very noticeable. It is only because the correctly gendered words are used for most people that they blend into the background.

Gendered terms and phrases are rarely correctly gendered for non-binary people, either referring to a single gender or both binary genders. In an isolated incident it could be considered a minor annoyance, or at worst mildly insulting, but when it is a constant everyday experience it wears down a person's mental health and leads to them feeling excluded from society.

It is a common misconception to assume that phrases covering both binary genders, such as 'ladies and gentlemen', are inclusive of everyone when, in fact, they ignore the existence of non-binary people. Truly inclusive language does exist, which doesn't refer to anyone's gender or use gendered terms, and this is what we mean when we describe gender-neutral language. This is actually commonly used already, although not as frequently as gendered language. Indeed, the vast majority of people don't notice the difference at all and it is unlikely that you have noticed its usage throughout this book.

Using gender-neutral language is very important to make non-binary people feel that they are a part of your organization and nothing is as readily noticeable to non-binary people as gendered language. Finding gender-neutral words to use is actually very easy, but what does require some effort is checking that you haven't defaulted to using gendered language. To help you get started Table 6.1 shows the most common words and phrases to watch out for and some suggestions or gender-neutral alternatives.

Table 6.1: Gender-neutral alternatives to common phrases

Gendered phrase	Gender-neutral alternative
He/she, (s)he, he or she	They
Ladies and gentlemen	Context-specific words such as (honoured) guests, (valued) customers
Hello sir/madam Dear sir/madam	Simply omit when used as a greeting and just use 'hello' To whom it may concern
Man/woman	Person

Getting gender-neutral language right does take time and requires a high level of attention to detail. We expect that you will make mistakes. When this does happen, fix it where you can and if someone has pointed it out to you, simply thank them and let them know that you'll continue trying in the future.

Inclusion policies

Our work has found that organizations' equality and diversity policies are not seen by non-binary people as good indicators of how inclusive an organization is. This is because they have become generic documents simply parroting legislative requirements and making no mention of non-binary people themselves. Many organizations have inclusion policies that are comprised of one line, stating that they 'are an equal opportunities employer and will comply with the law'. This tells the reader very little, as whether the organization states this or not, it is still bound by the law. Further than this it does not convey any information about what the organization is doing to make the workplace inclusive, as it is still possible to comply with the law and have an exclusionary environment. This is particularly true in the case of non-binary people where the law is not sufficient to tackle the issues they face.

For inclusion policies to add value they must be significantly improved upon. For an inclusion policy to have impact it must be authentic and personal, tailored to a particular organization. It should show your under-standing of the key issues facing groups, for example, knowledge of the gender pay gap or, for non-binary people the ability to record their genders correctly, and it should show what actions you have already taken or are planning on taking to resolve any problems. This will give a much clearer picture to anyone interested in working with you and allow you to showcase your work. Most importantly, an inclusion policy should explicitly state your support for minority groups, which could be done through a statement by senior management. It should also be updated regularly and seen as a living document, so that it remains up to date with the latest issues.

Good examples come from larger organizations that have dedicated equality and diversity and inclusion sections on their websites, or from political parties that demonstrate their support for minority voters. These provide a good structure but should not be copied word for word, otherwise the information simply becomes generic. As mentioned in the last chapter in relation to inclusive recruitment and retention policies, an effective inclusion policy can provide a key differentiator between yourself and competitors, helping you to attract and retain the best talent.

While it is important to focus on showcasing your own knowledge and work, the standard content of current inclusion policies should not be omitted. The policy should still cover your compliance with legal obligations and also detail your complaints procedure. These sections can remain generic if you have sufficiently demonstrated your own understanding and work, but should still be more detailed than a single line.

Inclusion policies are not currently seen as important indicators of an organization's inclusivity; however, this is a fault of the quality of policies rather than the principle. They should not be completely ignored but rather expanded on and brought up to a much higher standard. Once you've done this, it is worth publicizing your policy so that it will not be missed.

Single-gender services

Many services operate for single genders, providing tailored content and creating a more beneficial environment.

It is important to understand how non-binary people integrate into such services, in order to allow the services to continue functioning and benefiting as many people as possible. To achieve this it is not necessary to make any drastic changes to a service's model but simply give non-binary people the option to attend.

Non-binary people share many characteristics and experiences with binary men and women and would benefit from many of the tailored services. Unfortunately, due to the relatively small number of non-binary people, it is unlikely to be possible to offer specific non-binary services on a wide range of topics. To ensure that non-binary people are not disadvantaged they should be given the option to be included in current single-gender services.

To achieve this we have to communicate the fact that non-binary people are welcome at the service and provide them with enough information to be able to assess whether a particular service is appropriate for them. We recommend that it is explicitly stated that although the service is aimed at people of a specific gender, non-binary people are still welcome to attend. In addition, the way in which the service is tailored to people of a specific gender should be described. This might include discussions of specific experiences or the creation of a specific atmosphere.

Providers of single-gender services are frequently worried about the effects of including non-binary people and the reactions of other service users. As the provider it is important for you to ensure everyone at the service is welcomed, whatever type of person they may be. Negative reactions to non-binary people are usually based on a lack of knowledge and experience and it is up to the provider to bridge this gap. In any negative situation it is important to explain that the non-binary person has a right to attend and that they should be treated with courtesy. The provider should create the atmosphere at the service, and displaying a positive reaction to other people will go a long way towards avoiding negative incidents.

While many people view non-binary inclusion in single-gender services as a threat, this is not true and creating an inclusive environment for all is entirely possible.

Dress codes

Dress codes can represent a particular problem for non-binary people as they are frequently gendered, with different clothing sets for men and women. This may not suit non-binary people or may not allow them to express themselves as they would like. While media attention is focused on non-binary people who dress androgynously, or in a combination of hyper masculine and feminine styles simultaneously, most non-binary people do not dress significantly differently from other people.

Being able to express their gender through their attire is one of the major sources of worry for non-binary people about being open with regard to their gender identity, with 85 per cent experiencing some level of worry (Fernandez *et al.* 2017). This is because changing your style of dress can make you visibly different and many people have strongly negative reactions to those they perceive to be dressed inappropriately. Outcomes for those who were open about their gender identity were significantly more positive, and 50 per cent of non-binary people reported that their employer already had inclusive dress codes in place. This is frequently because dress codes remain unwritten, with standards set implicitly, or because only a general outline is given, such as 'businesswear'.

There is a distinct difference between reported experiences based on a person's sex assigned at birth in that people assigned female at birth (AFAB) have more positive experiences than people assigned male at birth (AMAB). This is due to the wider range of acceptable styles in what is termed 'womenswear' and stronger negative reactions to what people perceive as an inappropriately dressed man.

In order to establish an inclusive dress code it is important to focus on its purpose: that it should be professional and functional. When providing a detailed specification of dress codes, which include specific items of clothing, it is better to present these not as sets of clothing for women or men, but as options that anyone can choose from. For example, instead of specifying that women should wear skirts with black shoes and men should wear suits, these should be presented as: 'clothing set one includes a skirt with black shoes' and 'clothing set two includes suits'. Allowing some flexibility should be key to incorporating everyone's needs, and as long as the objectives are met the organization should not be overly controlling of its employees' dress.

When dress codes remain unwritten, it is important to communicate that you will support everyone in dressing in the style that suits them best, no matter what their gender identity is. This may be best placed within an inclusion policy, but it should not be positioned as solely for non-binary people, but should be for binary people as well. Similarly, when either a general outline or a more detailed specification is given, a note should be included in both instances that people should dress in the style that suits them best, as long as it meets the required standards.

Time off for medical treatment

Some, but not all non-binary people choose to undergo medical treatments as part of their transition and this may include a variety of procedures. The precise nature of the treatments they are undergoing should not affect their ability to perform their job and it should not be necessary for a company to know the details of these. Non-binary people may, however, require time off to attend medical appointments, or for recovery from medical procedures, and companies should make allowances if this is the case. Requests for time off for medical reasons should be treated in exactly the same way as they would for medical treatments required by other employees.

Unfortunately, it is common for people to ask intrusive, voyeuristic questions about non-binary people's medical status. While normally it would be considered exceptionally rude to ask the details of a person's medical treatment or questions about their body, it is too often assumed that these questions are acceptable when it comes to trans and non-binary people. At no stage should you ask for the details about a person's medical treatment.

In some cases it may be appropriate to know if medical procedures will impact a person's ability to perform their job. Requesting information should be kept strictly to a person's ability to perform actions, for example, the ability to lift heavy objects. In general, a non-binary person's ability to perform their job should not be impacted by any medical treatments and this should be taken as the initial assumption. If the medical treatment would impact their job, this is best discussed between the non-binary person and their doctor before informing their employer.

The time off needed for medical treatments may involve attending appointments or undergoing surgery with additional recovery time. It is worth noting that these are not considered elective procedures and are necessary for the continuing good health of the person. As such, this time off should be allowed by the company and it should not require the person to use their holiday allowance. Neither should a person be asked to disclose whether they will need time off for such treatments during a hiring process and it should not impact any other assessment of their performance. Any time off needed should be granted to the non-binary person at the time set by the relevant service, as it may not be possible to accommodate changes in dates.

CASE STUDY

A non-binary person approaches their manager and informs them that they are going to be undergoing some medical treatment, not specifying whether it is related to their gender or not. The non-binary person's job involves a mixture of heavy lifting and admin work. The time set for the medical treatment and recovery happens to fall into a very busy period for the company. How should the manager react? The manager has to be honest with the non-binary person, saying that this is a difficult time and that they are going to need some help from the non-binary person to plan around their treatment. The manager asks the non-binary person to discuss with their doctor what they will and won't be able to do during the recovery period. It turns out that while the non-binary person will not be able to perform the heavy lifting part of their job, they can still perform the admin work. The manager shifts the non-binary person's lifting work to other employees while the non-binary person takes on more admin work.

Pronouns

Using the correct pronouns for a person is a very basic idea, but one that can make a huge difference to non-binary people's lives. Just as it would be considered disrespectful – and in the worst case, bullying or harassment – to purposefully use the wrong name for someone, it is wrong to intentionally use the incorrect pronouns for someone. In previous chapters we've discussed why non-binary people use gender-neutral pronouns and what these pronouns might be, but how do we practically tackle this issue?

The first step is knowledge. Simply knowing that some people use gender-neutral pronouns and that they should be respected goes a long way. This can be done through specific diversity training, which we will cover later in the chapter. The next step is to understand what you need to know. You aren't expected to memorize all the gender-neutral pronouns and we know that this can be a daunting task. Neither are you expected to get it right all the time, but what you do need to do is to make an effort. This will involve learning to associate different pronouns with a person when they ask you to refer to them differently and to use gender-neutral pronouns when asked. Non-binary people will show more goodwill when mistakes are made if you are making an effort, but this does only go so far and you do need to get it right.

You must also use the correct pronouns for a person at all times including when they are not present, rather than just to their face. While this may sound obvious, many people unfortunately feel they can disregard the wishes of a non-binary person behind their back. There is a caveat here, however; there may be situations where a non-binary person asks you to use a different set of pronouns for them to the ones that they usually prefer. This might be for their own safety or simply because they do not want to disclose that they are non-binary. For example, while a non-binary person might feel comfortable using gender-neutral pronouns around their colleagues they may wish to use 'he' or 'she' around customers who may not be as inclusive. You should always ask the non-binary person if they would like to do this but should not pressure them into using specific pronouns; it would be discrimination to require them not to be visibly non-binary because you think it might damage your organization's image, or for any other reason.

There has been a growth of standard practices among organizations who are specifically attempting to be non-binary inclusive, such as charities. These practices include asking all people what their pronouns are when you first meet them, rather than assuming them; inevitably, people assume that someone's pronouns are either 'he' or 'she', which excludes non-binary people. This can still create a number of awkward conversations as the majority of people do not understand why you would be asking such a thing. You should only do this if you feel confident that you would be able to explain why you are asking.

The other common practice that has emerged is to pre-empt having to ask about pronouns by stating your own pronouns whenever you introduce yourself. This might include doing so in person or when signing emails or letters. Including your pronouns at the end of emails or letters is something that we would recommend adopting because, unlike the other spoken practices, it doesn't usually lead to any awkward conversations; the majority of binary people simply gloss over it, while it stands out for non-binary people. This practice also has the added benefit of removing any confusion for those with gender-neutral names such as Sam or Alex. The specific format can vary from person to person but a simple explanation underneath a name works well, for example:

Frank
He/him

The best way to implement this is to make it a normalized practice, starting with a small group of people who consistently use it, which leads to other people picking up on it and using it too. From experience, this way appears to have a higher adoption rate than explicitly asking everyone to start doing it.

CASE STUDY

A non-binary person approaches their manager and tells them that they would like to be referred to with the pronouns ze/hir from now on. How should the manager react? The manager lets the non-binary person know that they are not familiar with these pronouns but will try their best to get them right. They ask the non-binary person to be patient while they learn and to please correct them if ze notices any mistakes. The manager also asks hir

how ze would like to be referred to around clients
who may not be so inclusive. Both agree that it
would be best to just refer to the non-binary person
as ze/hir when clients are not present. Afterwards,
the manager practises using the correct pronouns to
get used to them.

Disclosure and Barring Service checks

Some types of work will require background checks
on employees to ensure that the work being carried
out remains safe, such as when working with children.
Unfortunately, some people still believe that non-binary, or
trans people in general, pose a specific threat to vulnerable
people, especially children. This is an unfortunate biased
and discriminatory view and has no basis. Non-binary
people can, and do, work with vulnerable people and they
should not be excluded from these positions.

Background checks, however, can be an issue for
trans and non-binary people as their full history must
be checked, including under any previous names. This
needs to be carried out in a way that is thorough, but
also maintains the privacy of the person being checked.
The Disclosure and Barring Service (DBS) in the UK
runs a specific service for sensitive applications that is
inclusive of trans people. The check will be carried out
by the DBS and the results passed to an employer, but
sensitive information about the person's history will not
be. The DBS can be contacted for further information
about this service.

In general, all information required for background
checks should be collected by a dedicated service and

not by an employer. Sensitive information, such as a person's previous name(s), should only be accessible to the background service provider and not to the employer. Should any issues arising out of the background checks have occurred under a previous name, these should be presented as arising under their current name, with the previous name omitted.

Pensions

Pensions remain a developing area for trans and non-binary people as some schemes have different structures based on the different life expectancies for men and women, with different retirement ages. The question of concern is which scheme a non-binary person should be placed in. This has been historically done based on a person's legal gender, even though this is incorrect for non-binary people.

This topic is becoming less of an issue, however, due to gendered pension schemes being phased out. To our knowledge, this does not affect private pension schemes that do not have gendered structures. The UK state pension scheme continues to have a gendered structure, although it is planned to equalize this by December 2018. If it is necessary to store data for this purpose for a non-binary person, it should be kept separately to their other records and be marked as confidential information.

In general, this remains an unclear area which may develop further in the future. The best current understanding of the system suggests that it is safest to place non-binary people in the gendered schemes that correspond to their legal gender. If the person's gender is legally recognized as non-binary, it would then be safest to include them in the scheme for their sex assigned at birth, although this should be discussed with the non-binary person first.

Genuine occupational requirements

Genuine occupational requirements (GORs) exist in UK law to allow key services to run that would otherwise not be able to do so under the Equality Act restrictions. They may require a specific type of person to perform a specific role, for example a Black and minority ethnic (BME) worker to provide support and advice to the BME community. Cases where this applies are relatively rare and they should not be considered a standard practice. In all cases they have to be fully justifiable. The most well-known cases of this being used relating to gender identity are women's refuges requiring workers to be cis women, although this is not universal among refuges.

GORs allow an exemption to the Equality Act provided that: the requirement is necessary for a job to be performed; it accomplishes a legitimate aim; and that the requirement is proportional to achieve the aim. A common criticism of the exemption is that it can allow scope for intrusive questioning of 'suspected' employees who may be trans, which may breach an employee's right to privacy, going against the European Convention on Human Rights (ECHR).

While the Gender Recognition Act has previously ensured employers could not discriminate against trans individuals on the grounds of occupational requirements, the current wording of the Equality Act allows for this regardless of a trans individual holding a GRC or not. There is a move to amend the Act so that occupational requirements concerning single-sex service provision should *not* apply to people who have a GRC, but it is unclear when or if this will take place in the near future.

For those services that do rely on GORs it is important to understand how non-binary people will fit into this system both to allow the services to continue and to avoid discriminating against non-binary people. This remains an unclear area because non-binary people are not formally recognized in UK law and there are no cases where their circumstances have been specifically referred to. Instead, they are partially included within all trans people. However, the introduction of legal recognition would likely drastically change this situation and require clarity on the subject.

Non-binary people are a very diverse group and share many characteristics with binary people. This makes it difficult to produce the clear-cut situations that are required for GORs where people's differences impact their work. We do not know of any situation where a non-binary person could not perform the same task as a binary person. Excluding all non-binary people from a job would be using too broad a brush, while attempting to split non-binary people based on some shared characteristic with binary people would be an unjust denial of the differences between the two groups.

Excluding non-binary people through a GOR would have to be exceptionally carefully assessed and we do not envision this to have positive or fair outcomes. We recommend that GORs should not be used to exclude non-binary people. Instead, what the job would involve and the pressures surrounding it should be clearly described, which would allow non-binary people to make their own judgement about their suitability for the job.

Since we are discussing the exclusion of a minority group rather than a majority group, the dynamics involved are different and we believe that self-selection would produce the correct group to allow services to function effectively. Since the number of non-binary people is relatively few, any approach will likely have only a minor impact. Without any supporting evidence we believe it would be wrong to choose to exclude people as the default, and it is this lack of evidence that stops us from being more decisive on an issue that will remain a developing area.

Training

Employee training is an important part of any equality and diversity strategy but even more so when it comes to non-binary people. The primary cause of exclusionary or discriminatory incidents is a lack of knowledge about who non-binary people are, rather than them happening out of malice. To combat this, basic training on non-binary people is essential and should be included alongside other equality and diversity training. This is best provided for all new employees, with refresher courses at appropriate intervals for current employees, rather than only being provided once an incident has occurred.

Explaining non-binary identities in an accessible and simple manner is a complicated thing to do, due to the wide range of issues this encompasses and the academic style in which these issues are usually discussed. We don't recommend that you attempt to build your own training session entirely from scratch as you may be at risk of confusing the situation rather than making it clearer.

We do recommend using the previous chapters of this book as a basis for your own training as they cover the key information needed to build a working understanding of non-binary people. Rather than providing you with a generic training document as part of this book, we have sought to provide the components for you to put into your own training; this is because training that is tailored to your own organization will have a higher impact than generic materials, and creating your own training serves as an important learning exercise to improve your knowledge. The data sources that we have used to create our figures as well as our terminology glossary are contained at the back of this book.

However, there is never any substitute for training delivered by specialist organizations, that will be able to respond comprehensively to any questions arising from the training and provide further support where necessary. Unfortunately, training on non-binary people remains a gap in the offering of many charities, and those that do offer it have, historically, needed to make some serious improvements. Where possible, training is best delivered by non-binary, focused organizations, of which there are a growing number in the UK and around the world.

Informing co-workers

For those non-binary people who wish to change their name, style of dress or be referred to by different pronouns, informing others of these changes can be stressful and nerve-racking. Doing this puts them in a vulnerable position, relying on others to respect them and treat them correctly, although, unfortunately, many people refuse to do so. This can become a significant issue in the workplace, where people must continue to interact with each other in a cooperative fashion.

We need to make this process as smooth as possible to get the best outcomes for everyone. This includes considering who to inform, when to do so and what information to pass along, as well as follow-up to ensure there are no issues. This cannot be a rigid framework but must be done with the full involvement of the non-binary person, at the same time ensuring they retain control over the process. As a first step we expect the non-binary person to inform their manager, or a person responsible for HR, who will then assist in informing other relevant co-workers. It is significantly less common for the non-binary person to inform everyone themselves as this process is easier with support from management.

It is important to pass the right information to the right people, as otherwise this can lead to confusion or to a situation where these changes are sensationalized. We recommend viewing this as a re-introduction made to the people who already know the non-binary person. Simply inform them of the person's change of name, or pronouns, and let them know that they should use these from now on. This should be treated as a routine matter, announced in the same way that any other staff matter would be, but only to the people who already know the non-binary person. The format of how this is done should be that preferred by the non-binary person; this may be by management in person, by email or by the non-binary person themselves if they wish.

To make this process smoother it can be helpful for it to be done while the non-binary person is away, allowing co-workers the time to adjust and giving them a clear starting point from which the changes will come into effect. Non-binary people, however, should not be forced to take any unpaid or holiday leave for this to take place.

If you have provided training on non-binary people as part of wider equality and diversity training, then there should be little need for extra questions from co-workers; however, it is good practice to provide them with a point of contact for further explanation. This task shouldn't fall on the non-binary person themselves, unless they feel entirely comfortable taking this on.

Throughout this process the wishes of the non-binary person should come first, and while we can give some guidelines, their choice should always be final. The most important part of this process is to communicate to everyone that the non-binary person has the full support of management and the company, as this will set the tone for everyone else.

Chapter 7

Closing Remarks

Despite being part of human history for thousands of years, non-binary people are often ignored and forgotten in our modern society. Life can be difficult when you are non-binary and forced to justify your own existence, navigate barriers to access basic services or become the victim of violence. There is no reason for these things to happen – they are problems we all create and which we are all responsible for fixing.

We hope this book has been a source of guidance for you, even if coming into it you didn't know much about trans people at all, and even less about non-binary people specifically! Please keep asking questions, challenging yourself and others, and talking directly to employees who may be affected, positively or negatively, by steps you take to become more inclusive.

What is most important is keeping an open mind and carrying on this discussion. We would encourage you to share your learning from this in a session for all to attend, or find other ways of encouraging employees on all levels to think about some of the case studies presented in this book and the questions they raise. Are individuals doing enough to support non-binary colleagues? What would they say before/after reading this if a colleague came out to them as non-binary, or wanted to use different pronouns at work? How would they support someone who has changed their name, or is being bullied at work because they are non-binary? Making these topics something that is not just confined to a single equality and diversity training session is important to make the lessons stick.

However, the steps towards making the workplace an inclusive environment shouldn't just stop at the ideas suggested here. As well as implementing changes, such as looking at uniform policies, reviewing data storage and thinking about gender-neutral bathrooms, many organizations are going above and beyond by actively celebrating gender diversity in the workplace. What can organizations do to mark Trans Day of Visibility annually, and how can the inclusion and celebration of non-binary people be incorporated into this? How can non-binary inclusion become part of LGBT+ celebrations more visibly? When designing images or writing resources, is the inclusion of non-binary people considered?

So, to recap, what makes a workplace inclusive of non-binary people? Some of the practical steps that can be taken are:

- understanding the things that non-binary people want to see in employers – respect for pronouns, options for gender-neutral titles and gender options on forms and records, gender-neutral bathrooms and inclusive dress codes

- ensuring staff networks are focused on providing a space for non-binary staff members

- ensuring inclusion policies explicitly mention non-binary people and making it clear that any transphobic harassment of employees by staff, customers or clients won't be tolerated

- ensuring the organization is up to speed with legislation that impacts non-binary people, such as having an understanding of the Gender Recognition Act, the Equality Act and the Data Protection Act

- introducing equality and diversity training that covers non-binary issues as a standard item and which is rolled out to all members of staff.

Some of these steps may seem daunting; however, they don't all have to be done in one go. Concentrate on one or two issues first and then think about a structured way to roll out all recommendations gradually. Ultimately, taking these steps will not just make the workplace more inclusive of non-binary people, but will ensure that all staff, regardless of who they are, will be better supported.

While non-binary people's legal status in many countries is still a grey area, the future is brighter. There is a significant movement towards legal recognition of non-binary genders and better protection from anti-discrimination laws. Several countries have already forged ahead in this and the overall question is one of when these changes will occur rather than if.

We hope that by reading this book you've gained a better understanding of who non-binary people are and the challenges they face. We hope that you will move forward with making your own organization more inclusive, not just because it makes sense from a business perspective but because it will have a wider impact throughout society. In the end we'd like to thank you for being part of the solution.

Glossary

To respect someone's gender identity, you don't have to learn any words off by heart, or get anxious about using 'correct' phrasing. However, we do use some specific words in this book that you may want clarification on. Below is a selection of terms explaining different genders, pronouns and legislation that are useful to know. For further information or if you're looking for a term that isn't described here or in this book, there are lots of resources that can help you online, as more and more people are writing up their experiences of being non-binary. We recommend reading the stories on the Beyond the Binary website (http://beyondthebinary.co.uk) to help you understand the diversity of experiences and ways of identifying.

AFAB (ASSIGNED FEMALE AT BIRTH) those whose sex was listed as female on their birth certificate at the time of their birth.

AGENDER the gender identity of someone who is without gender; agender people may or may not alter their appearances to reflect their lack of gender, and may or may not identify as trans. 'Gender neutral' can be another term for agender.

AMAB (ASSIGNED MALE AT BIRTH) those whose sex was listed as male on their birth certificate at the time of their birth.

ANDROGYNOUS someone who presents in a mixture of feminine and masculine styles.

BIGENDER someone whose gender identity encompasses both male and female.

BINARISM the belief or practices that promote binary genders as better or more valid than non-binary genders. The assumption that everyone holds a binary gender.

BINARY the two genders of man and woman (or male and female) are commonly referred to as binary genders.

CISNORMATIVITY the assumption that everyone is cisgender, and/or the view that cisgender is the default gender, that is, it is 'normal'.

CISSEXISM the belief or practices that promote being cisgender as better or more valid than being transgender or being non-binary.

DEADNAMING a 'deadname' is the birth name of someone who has since changed their name; deadnaming is calling someone by that deadname (this can be deliberate or unintentional).

DEMI-GENDER a person with a demi-gender may be part or mostly one gender and part or mostly one of another. For example, a demi-boy may be someone who is mostly a boy, but can be part of something else.

DYADIC adjective to describe someone who is not intersex.

ENBY a shorthand term for 'non-binary' (from the initials NB). Often used by younger non-binary people.

FTM an outdated term for someone who transitions from female to male. Its usage is now discouraged.

GENDER/GENDER IDENTITY a collection of socially constructed categories that people use to describe their own experiences or their own sense of self.

GENDER DYSPHORIA gender dysphoria is a medical condition defined as clinical distress (the opposite of euphoria) in response to being treated as a different gender than the one you are.

GENDER EXPRESSION how someone expresses their gender through mannerism or styles of dress.

GENDER-NEUTRAL adjective describing anything that is without gender or encompasses all genders.

GENDER REASSIGNMENT a medical and legal term for the processes that make up transition.

GENDER RECOGNITION CERTIFICATE a legal document that changes a person's birth certificate from their sex assigned at birth. This was instated with the Gender Recognition Act 2004.

GENDERFLUID someone whose identity fluctuates between two or more genders.

GENDERQUEER a gender similar to 'non-binary', and sometimes used as an umbrella term to describe all people outside the binary genders of male and female.

INTERSEX an umbrella term for anyone who is born with genitalia, reproductive organs, sex hormone levels, gonads and/ or chromosomes that are inconsistent with the strictly defined male and female sex categories.

MICROAGGRESSION encompasses the daily comments, sleights and barriers that any marginalized group faces but which may not be considered discrimination under the law.

MISGENDER/MISPRONOUN to call someone by the wrong gender/gender pronoun/gendered term (this can be deliberate or unintentional).

MTF an outdated term for someone who transitions from male to female. Its usage is now discouraged.

MX a common title used by non-binary people in place of Mr or Ms.

NEUTROIS someone who identifies as being without gender.

NON-BINARY an umbrella term for anyone whose gender identity is not solely or completely described by the terms 'man' or 'woman'.

PRONOUNS how a person is referred to in the third person, for example, he, she, they.

PROTECTED CHARACTERISTIC a term in UK law to describe being a member of certain marginalized groups. Listed in the Equality Act 2010.

SEX a classification of male or female (or intersex) based on a person's anatomy and gendered physical traits or chromosomes. Used as a loose grouping of physical characteristics.

SEX ASSIGNED AT BIRTH the sex noted down at a person's birth, usually based on their genital configuration. It is very rare for this to be anything other than male or female, with intersex people forcible and arbitrarily assigned one of these as well.

THIRD GENDER often used regionally in countries that are not European; this may refer to a culture-specific gender classification for trans people.

TRANS/TRANSGENDER an umbrella term to encompass all those who are a different gender from what was assigned to them at birth. This commonly includes non-binary people as well as trans men and women.

TRANS FEMININE someone who was AMAB and who identifies as or has transitioned to a more feminine gender. Often problematically used as an umbrella term for all AMAB trans people.

TRANS MASCULINE someone who was AFAB and who identifies as or has transitioned to a more masculine gender. Often problematically used as an umbrella term for all AFAB trans people.

TRANSITION a process by which someone seeks to better align aspects of their life with their gender identity, for example, by changing their gender expression through wearing different clothes. Transitioning may or may not also include medical and legal aspects, for example, medical treatments, or changing identity documents to reflect one's gender identity.

TRANSMISOGYNY discrimination or bigotry towards trans women and feminine non-binary people.

TRANSPHOBIA discrimination or hatred of trans and non-binary people.

TRANSSEXUAL an outdated term for binary trans people.

TWO-SPIRIT Native Americans who have specific and sacred gender roles that may be outside of male and female, masculine and feminine, and/or a combination of both.

References

Action for Trans Health (2014) #transdocfail: moving forward with a new non-binary protocol [Blog post]. Accessed on 19/08/2017 at http://actionfortranshealth.org.uk/2014/10/20/transdocfail-moving-forward-with-a-new-non-binary-protocol

Action for Trans Health (2015) *Non-Binary Experiences of Healthcare.* Action for Trans Health. Accessed on 13/08/17 at http://actionfortranshealth.org.uk/wp-content/uploads/2015/02/gender-id.pdf

Aspinall, P.J. (2009) *Estimating the Size and Composition of the LGBT Population in Britain.* Research Report 37. Manchester: Equality and Human Rights Commission. Accessed on 12/08/17 at www.equalityhumanrights.com/sites/default/files/research-report-37-estimating-lesbian-gay-and-bisexual-population-in-britain.pdf

Beyond the Binary (2015a) #SpecificDetriment: what you told us [Blog post]. Beyond the Binary. Accessed on 31/08/17 at http://beyondthebinary.co.uk/specificdetriment-what-you-told-us

Beyond the Binary (2015b) *Non-Binary Gender Identity Survey.* Beyond the Binary. Accessed on 31/08/17 at http://beyondthebinary.co.uk/non-binary-gender-identity-survey

Chakraborti, N., and Hardy, S.J. (2015) *LGB&T Hate Crime Reporting: Identifying Barriers and Solutions.* Manchester: Equality and Human Rights Commission. Accessed on 13/08/17 at www.equalityhumanrights.com/sites/default/files/research-lgbt-hate-crime-reporting-identifying-barriers-and-solutions.pdf

Data Protection Act (1998) Chapter 29. Accessed on 24/09/17 at www.legislation.gov.uk/ukpga/1998/29/contents

Equality Act (2010) Chapter 15. Accessed on 24/09/17 at www.legislation.gov.uk/ukpga/2010/15/contents

Fernandez, J., Gibson, S., and Twist, J. (2017) *Non-Binary Workplace and Customer Experience Survey.* Beyond the Binary. Accessed on 31/08/17 at http://beyondthebinary.co.uk/wp-content/uploads/2017/03/Non-binary-Workplace-and-Customer-Experience-Survey-1.pdf

Gender Recognition Act (2004) Chapter 7. Accessed on 24/09/17 at www.legislation.gov.uk/ukpga/2004/7/contents

Glen, F. and Hurrell, K. (2012) *Technical Note: Measuring Gender Identity.* Manchester: Equality and Human Rights Commission. Accessed on 13/08/17 at www.equalityhumanrights.com/en/publication-download/technical-note-measuring-gender-identity

Grammaticus, S. (12th century) *Gesta Danorum.* Accessed on 24/09/17 at www.sacred-texts.com/neu/saxo/saxo06.htm

J. Walter Thompson Intelligence (2016) Study of youth attitudes towards gender. New York: J. Walter Thompson Company. Accessed on 13/08/17 at www.jwtintelligence.com/2016/03/gen-z-goes-beyond-gender-binaries-in-new-innovation-group-data

Mitchell, M., and Howarth, C. (2009) *Trans Research Review.* Accessed on 19/08/2017 at www.equalityhumanrights.com/sites/default/files/research_report_27_trans_research_review.pdf

Nonbinary Stats (2016) Nonbinary/genderqueer survey 2016 [Blog post]. Accessed on 12/08/17 at http://nonbinarystats.tumblr.com/post/141316036775/nbgq-survey-2016-the-uk-results

Office for National Statistics (2011) 2011 United Kingdom Census data. Office for National Statistics. Accessed on 13/08/17 at www.ons.gov.uk/peoplepopulationandcommunity/culturalidentity/religion/articles/religioninenglandandwales2011/2012-12-11

Petitions UK Government and Parliament (2015) Allow transgender people to self-define their legal gender. Accessed on 19/08/2017 at https://petition.parliament.uk/petitions/104639

Pierce, C. M. (1970) 'Offensive Mechanisms.' In F. Barbour (ed.) *The Black Seventies*. Boston, MA: Porter Sargent.

Royal College of General Practitioners Northern Ireland (RCGPNI) (2015) *Guidelines for the Care of Trans Patients in Primary Care*. Belfast: RCGPNI. Accessed on 13/08/17 at www.rcgp.org.uk/policy/rcgp-policy-areas/lgbt.aspx

Sunil Babu Pant and Others v Nepal Government and Others (2007) Accessed on 19/08/2017 at http://icj.wpengine.netdna-cdn.com/wp-content/uploads/2012/07/Sunil-Babu-Pant-and-Others-v.-Nepal-Government-and-Others-Supreme-Court-of-Nepal.pdf

Stonewall (2017) *A Vision for Change: Acceptance without Exception for Trans People*. London: Stonewall. Accessed on 12/08/17 at www.stonewall.org.uk/sites/default/files/stw-vision-for-change-2017.pdf.

Stonewall (2017a) *Stonewall's Top 100 Employees*. Accessed on 24/09/17 at www.stonewall.org.uk/workplace-equality-index

The Daily Dot (2017) '"Nonbinary" is now a legal gender, Oregon court rules.' Accessed on 19/08/2017 at www.dailydot.com/irl/oregon-court-rules-non-binary-gender-legal

Titman, N. (2014a) When was the Mx gender-inclusive title created? Practical Androgeny. Accessed on 12/08/17 at https://practicalandrogyny.com/2014/08/28/when-was-the-mx-gender-inclusive-title-created

Titman, N. (2014b) How many people in the United Kingdom are nonbinary? Practical Androgeny. Accessed on 12/08/17 at https://practicalandrogyny.com/2014/12/16/how-many-people-in-the-uk-are-nonbinary

Valentine, V. (2016a) *Non-Binary People's Experiences in the UK*. Edinburgh: Scottish Transgender Alliance. Accessed on 12/08/17 at www.scottishtrans.org/wp-content/uploads/2016/08/Report-final.pdf

Valentine, V. (2016b) *Non-Binary People's Experiences of Using UK Gender Identity Clinics*. Edinburgh: Scottish Transgender Alliance. Accessed on 12/08/17 at www.scottishtrans.org/wp-content/uploads/2016/11/Non-binary-GIC-mini-report.pdf

Whittle, S., Turner, L. and Al-Alami, M. (2007) *Engendered Penalties: Transgender and Transsexual People's Experiences of Inequality and Discrimination*. A research report and project commissioned by the Equalities Review. Wetherby: Communities and Local Government Publications.

Women and Equalities Committee (2015) Oral evidence: Transgender Equality Inquiry. Accessed on 26/08/17 at http://data.parliament. uk/writtenevidence/committeeevidence.svc/evidencedocument/ women-and-equalities-committee/transgender-equality/oral/23159. html

Women and Equalities Committee (2016) *Transgender Equality: First Report of Session 2015–16*. London: The Stationary Office. Accessed on 13/08/17 at https://publications.parliament.uk/pa/cm201516/ cmselect/cmwomeq/390/390.pdf

World Professional Association for Transgender Health (WPATH) (2011) *Standards of Care for the Health of Transsexual, Transgender, and Gender-Nonconforming People*. Version 7. Accessed on 19/08/2017 at https://s3.amazonaws.com/amo_hub_content/Association140/files/ Standards%20of%20Care%20V7%20-%202011%20WPATH%20 (2)(1).pdf

Yeung, P. (2016) 'Transphobic hate crimes in "sickening" 170% rise as low prosecution rates create "lack of trust" in police.' *Independent*. 28 July. Accessed on 19/08/2017 at www.independent.co.uk/news/uk/home-news/transphobic-hate-crime-statistics-violence-transgender-uk-police-a7159026.html

Index